GirlForceshine

First published in Australia in 2006 by ABC Books for the Australian Broadcasting Corporation
Published in the United States in 2010 by Bloomsbury U.S.A. Children's Books
175 Fifth Avenue, New York, New York 10010

Library of Congress Cataloging-in-Publication Data
Goldstein, Nikki.
GirlForceshine / by Nikki Goldstein. — 1st U.S. ed.
p.   cm.
ISBN 978-1-59990-355-2
1. Beauty, Personal. 2. Teenage girls—Health and hygiene. 3. Grooming for girls. I. Title.
RA777.25.G65 2010   613´.04243—dc22   2009013019

First U.S. Edition January 2010
Printed in China by C&C Offset Printing Co. Ltd., Shenzhen, Guangdong
10 9 8 7 6 5 4 3 2 1

All papers used by Bloomsbury U.S.A. are natural, recyclable products made from wood grown in
well-managed forests. The manufacturing processes conform to the environmental regulations of
the country of origin.

Photography by Steven Chee (except as noted below)
Design by Lucy Isherwood for Litmus Design and Nerida Orsatti for Nerida Orsatti Design
Illustrations by Lucy Isherwood and Nerida Orsatti
Color reproduction by PageSet, Sydney

Additional picture credits
Page 60: Monkey Business Images
Page 76: Jupiter Images Corporation
Page 92: Stockbyte/Getty Images
Page 102: iStockphoto.com/Jason Stitt
Page 134: Stockbyte/Getty Images
Page 147: Stockbyte/Getty Images
Pages 160-161: Monkey Business Images

NIKKI GOLDSTEIN

GirlForce*shine*

A Girl's Guide to TOTAL BEAUTY

BLOOMSBURY

NEW YORK BERLIN LONDON

Contents

Discover

your Beauty Type—go on,
allow yourself to shine!

CHAPTER ONE

Wanna love the skin you're in? It's easy. Simply stop comparing yourself with everyone else. It doesn't matter if you have zits, small boobs, a big butt, hopeless hair, whatever—we all have parts we think are less than perfect. The point is to embrace yourself as a whole person inside and out. It's time to accept yourself, celebrate your unique beauty, and say sayonara to negative self-talk.

This book isn't about trying to get a celebrity bod or torturing yourself because you don't look like Blake Lively. It is about getting gorgeous—making the best of what nature gave YOU and celebrating YOUR unique look. Beauty is the inner glow you get from being okay with yourself—just the way you are.

You wanted a beauty book that was all your own. Well, now you've got it.

Teen beauty concerns are NOT the same as anyone else's. Your hormones are surging, your skin breaks out, your hair won't do what it's supposed to do (let's not get started about the other kind of hair), and you're sprouting breasts (or not). In **Shine**, you'll learn how to make the most of your assets so you can feel confident every day. Get ready to look and feel great.

I'm not going to tell you it's possible to transform yourself into the hottest girl on the planet overnight, but what I am going to do is share tons of inside info that I've learned as a beauty editor from some of the world's best hair and make-up artists, beauty consultants, and doctors.

Believe me, when you get a handle on these professional tips and techniques (and I promise that'll be in a flash), you'll feel confident enough to walk out the door every day with your head held high.

Every time you pamper yourself—

by washing your hair, putting on a face mask,

applying yummy lip gloss, or doing your nails—

you'll unleash GirlForce.

Why? Because when you take time to take care of yourself and behave in a loving way, you release feel-good vibes that translate into vitality and energy. That vitality and energy is GirlForce.

SO READ ON

and discover your Beauty Type.

Your Beauty Type is an extension of your Body Type, which you may have discovered by reading *GirlForce: A Girl's Guide to the Body and Soul* (you can also check it out on www.MyGirlForce.com). Once you know your Beauty Type and its unique set of characteristics, you'll have access to a secret universe of info and advice for virtually every beauty problem you can imagine.

The magic of Ayurveda—the 5,000-year-old "science of life" from India that inspires GirlForce—is that it has a solution for everything from zits and greasy hair to what perfume or eye shadow colors will improve your mood and balance your body, mind, and spirit.

The more you're aware of how your Beauty Type "flavors" your skin, energy, hair, moods, personality—in fact, everything about you—the more you'll be able to take advantage of the remedies, tips, and techniques in this book. Cool, huh? So take the following quiz and discover whether you're an Air, Fire, or Earth Beauty Type.

As you go through the test, circle the answer that most closely resembles you—a, b, or c. Only circle one answer per question, even if you feel you fall somewhere between two answers. At the end of each section, add up the number of a's, b's, and c's. The highest number of a's, b's, or c's should reveal your Beauty Type and will help you use this book.

Once you know your Beauty Type you'll be able to go straight to the remedies, tips, and techniques that are right for you.

Ready to get into it?

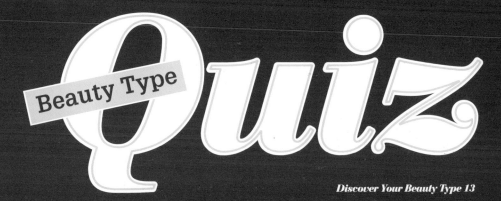

Beauty Type *Quiz*

2. Your coloring?
a) Dark for my race, tending to olive and brown undertones
b) Reddish undertones and sometimes freckles
c) Pale for my race

1. Your skin?
a) Dry
b) Normal/sensitive
c) Oily

3. Your face shape?
a) Small, thin, long, oval shaped
b) Heart shaped with sharp contours
c) Large and round or square with soft contours

4. Your hair color?
a) Dark brown or black
b) Blonde or red, sometimes chestnut
c) Dark blonde or brunette

5. Your hair texture?
a) Dry, kinky, frizzy, hard to manage
b) Soft and fine
c) Thick, wavy, oily

6. Your lips?
a) Fine, tend to be dry and a little uneven
b) Medium, soft, and red
c) Full, large, and even shaped

7. Your eyes?
a) Brown and small in comparison to my other features, with fine lashes and eyebrows
b) Sharp, bright, and intense, medium-size in comparison to my other features, with defined eyebrows
c) Deep blue or brown, large in comparison to my other features, with thick lashes and eyebrows

8. Your energy?
a) Comes and goes. I get tired easily
b) I have good energy reserves
c) Can be slow to get going, but once I start moving I have good stamina

9. Your temperature gauge?
a) I hate dry, windy, cold days and crave the sun
b) Crisp cool days suit me just fine because I burn up in summer
c) I don't like damp, cold weather

10. Your appetite?
a) I can take or leave food; I can eat any old time
b) I can set a watch by my tummy rumbles
c) I like my food, but I'm rarely starving

11. Your personal characteristics?
a) Adventurous, curious, original, exciting, charming
b) Passionate, challenging, stimulating, powerful
c) Stable, kind, deep, faithful, serene, compassionate

12. Your talents?
a) Innovative and creative
b) Good leader and decision maker
c) Nurturing and imaginative

13. Your memory?
a) I have the memory of an ant; I don't hold on to things for long
b) Quick, sharp; I'm good at cramming for an exam
c) I'm good at remembering things, even if they happened a long time ago

14. Your sleep?
a) I sleep very lightly and have lots of dreams, sometimes waking up during the night
b) I sleep soundly, but when I'm awake I'm awake
c) I sleep deep and long

Are you an

air, fire, or earth
BEAUTY TYPE?

If you scored mostly a's, you're a creative and cool Air Beauty Type. If you scored mostly b's, you're a sassy and sexy Fire Beauty Type, and if you scored mostly c's, you're a laid-back and luscious Earth Beauty Type.

No matter what shape or size your body is, no matter what color hair or skin you have, this book is about celebrating the unique qualities of all three Beauty Types. When you know your Beauty Type, you'll open a new door to self-acceptance and self-esteem. You'll stop comparing yourself with others and you'll learn how to balance your body, mind, and soul with the Beauty Type—balancing remedies, pampering therapies, tips, and inside info in this book. Go, girl!

It's rare, but if you came out as a different Beauty Type from your Body Type (see *GirlForce: A Girl's Guide to the Body and Soul* or www.MyGirlForce.com), it's possible you're a bit out of balance right now. Follow all the suggestions in this book for the Beauty Type your results showed in this quiz. Remember, everyone is different and unique and you're going to learn how to rock your own brand of beauty.

Mostly A's

Air girls are renowned for their distinctive beauty. Your face is probably not girl-next-door pretty, but you have a fascinating beauty that's stamped with individuality.

You're an Air Beauty Type

Your face tends to be small and your eyes quick, taking in a complete picture in a millisecond. You're likely to be either very tall like Paris Hilton or petite like Jada Pinkett-Smith. Air chicks have kinky hair that can be dry, and your skin, which is generally clear, can also be a bit dry. One of Air's signatures is cute little teeth that can be slightly crooked à la Kate Moss.

Sensitive Air girls, who are rarely outgoing cheerleader types, can sometimes feel a little geeky and worry that their quirky looks are less than perfect. When you learn how to celebrate the beauty of your unique looks and style, you emit an irresistible glow.

Beauty concerns: dry, fine, kinky hair; dry skin; brittle nails; lack of beauty confidence; very large or very small feet; big boobs or late-to-develop/small boobs; often very tall or very short.

Air girl

You shine with your unusual eye-catching features; clear skin; fine pores; cute lips and teeth; exciting energy; unique, eclectic, and sometimes edgy fashion style; and sparkling eyes.

Fire girl

You shine with your strong athletic build, great mane of hair, piercing eyes, good teeth and open smile, confidence, and chic fashion style.

Fire girls are the confident go-getters who are used to walking into a room and grabbing everyone's attention. Eva Mendes, Lindsay Lohan, and Rihanna are Fire girls who know how to stay in the spotlight.

Mostly B's

You're a Fire Beauty Type

Fire girls are mostly medium builds with an athletic shape. You can put on and take off weight pretty quickly when you exercise and eat right for your Body Type.

Your hair is a big part of your signature style. Your lush locks are often tinted with red highlights or undertones.

You blush easily and your skin is often warm to the touch. If you stay out in the sun, you can burn to a crisp. If you're out of balance, you might get red, angry zits or rashes that can dampen your confidence. When you feel good about yourself, you're one in a million.

Your eyes reflect your beauty with more than just their shape or color—the fact is that you really look at people when they speak to you and this ability to hold their gaze gives you mega-confidence.

Beauty concerns: rashes, red zits, soft hair that can be unmanageable, strong-smelling perspiration, getting overheated in summer.

Earth girl

You shine with your large eyes; glistening white teeth; super-wattage smile; feminine charms; slow, graceful moves; voluptuous bod; and classic fashion style.

Mostly C's

You're an Earth Beauty Type

The first thing people notice about Earth babes is their femininity: large eyes, white teeth, and lush hair. The Earth girl is the voluptuous diva who knows slow and steady wins the race.

Earth girls, like Beyoncé, are ample and babelicious. Your frame is generally considered large and you may tower over the guys you like. But that's no reason to worry; confidence will carry you a long way.

You tend to put on weight, especially around your hips and butt, yet when you celebrate your curvy bod and get into the lushness of your features, you develop bulletproof self-esteem.

Earth girls can tend to get slightly greasy hair and skin. Deep, under-the-skin pimples can be one of your major beauty concerns. Like Earth girls Jennifer Hudson and America Ferrera, your thick hair and full lips give you an exotic beauty that you call all your own.

Earth girls have a sensuous beauty and their graceful moves attract tons of admirers—although often they're not even aware of it.

Beauty concerns: greasy hair and skin, deep pimples, tendency to put on weight and difficulty in losing it.

If you've read *GirlForce: A Girl's Guide to the Body and Soul*, you already know that every single person on the planet has the elemental-energies Air, Fire, and Earth in their bodies and minds.

Air governs the lungs, the intellect, the holes and cavities in the body, the nervous system, the circulation, and the breath. Fire controls our impulses for hunger and thirst, the luster of the eyes and skin, the blood and the digestive system, and the balance of our body temperature. Earth governs all the fluids in the body, controls sleep as well as strength and stamina, and gives structure to the body in the form of our tissues and muscles.

No one is pure Air, pure Fire, or pure Earth; all of us are made up of the three different elements and they control all the vital functions of the body and mind. What makes us individuals, however, is the unique mix of those three elements in our bodies. Even though you and your best bud might be Fire girls, a quick glance in the mirror will tell you that although you may share loads of traits (you both get irritated when you're hungry, you both get sunburned when you spend too much time outdoors, and you both have a similar approach to life), you are not identical.

Be Beauty Type *beautiful*

In most people one elemental-energy—Air, Fire, or Earth—will dominate. (You can easily see that you have a mixture of all three elemental-energies in your body by looking back at your Beauty Type Quiz. Unless you got 100 percent from one elemental-energy, which would be incredibly rare, you'll notice that you also had a splash of the other two elements as well.)

If you scored equally over two elemental-energies, you may be a two-element Beauty Type. That's cool; the way to get the most out of this book is to read through all the info and tips and techniques on both types and pick the ones that seem most relevant at the time. As a two-element Beauty Type you'll notice that sometimes you'll feel one elemental-energy dominating and sometimes you'll feel the other.

For example, if you found you had equal amounts of Fire and Air, you'd discover that the Fire in you feels stronger on hot days and the Air elemental-energy in you would come out on cold, windy days. (For more info on how to balance your Body Type, check out *GirlForce: A Girl's Guide to the Body and Soul*.)

The point of knowing your Beauty Type is that it gives you a tried-and-tested ancient formula to balance your skin, body, and hair as well as your moods and emotions. You'll see that even though you're unique and precious as an individual (there will never be anyone else like YOU), you're also part of a club—you share your beauty concerns with millions of other girls.

The more you balance your Beauty Type, the better you'll feel and the hotter you'll look. It's a way of polishing and perfecting your appearance and it's also a way of connecting to your spirit—your GirlForce. Turn your everyday routines into a meditation of self-love and WOW, in next to no time you'll blast everyone away with your confidence and sassy style.

I hope you love this book as much as I loved writing it!

Nikki

CHAPTER TWO

Skin fitness

GREAT SKIN BASICS FOR EVERY TYPE

The secret of healthy-looking skin is health itself. When you balance your Beauty Type with the right foods, a little exercise, and plenty of pampering and nourishing routines, your skin will look and feel soft, smooth, and zit-free.

Wanna know more?

It gives away your emotions (like how you blush with embarrassment when you catch a glimpse of your crush or go pale with shock when you see him hanging out with a new girl). It also reveals a lot about how your bodily systems are functioning. If you're living on junk food, your skin is going to look, well, like you're living on junk food—it'll be dull, lackluster, and blotchy. If you skip gym class and allow your overall fitness to slump, your skin fitness will also suffer—it'll become sluggish, irritated, and patchy. And if you're buckling under life's pressures and feeling badly stressed out, your skin will also be stressed out. (It's no accident that you get more zits around exam time.)

The good news is, the reverse is also true. When you feel good about yourself and the world, and you're filled with the happiness-boosting powers of GirlForce, your skin positively glows. To create harmony that's reflected in your skin you need a holistic approach. That means taking your whole self into account:

mind, body, spirit & emotions.

Your Beauty Type reveals loads about your total self—physically and psychologically. Air Beauty Types, who are active, airy, and creative, tend to have dry skin and hair. Fire girls, who are passionate and intense, tend to have fiery skin that can be sensitive and prone to redness. Earth Beauty Types, who are serene, grounded, and laid-back, mostly have slightly thick, oily skin and hair.

KNOWING YOUR BEAUTY TYPE, and understanding how to balance it every day, will help you maintain a healthy glowing complexion; soft, manageable hair; strong, healthy nails; and bulletproof self-confidence.

AIR SKIN

PRESCRIPTION

- Eat lots of warm, grounding foods including root veggies such as sweet potatoes, beets, and parsnips to balance your digestive system and keep your skin clear and bright.

- Eat good oils such as olive oil to keep your skin lush.

- Snack on nuts such as walnuts; they contain vital nutrients for your skin.

- Add fish to your weekly menu; they contain omega-3 fatty acids, which quell the inflammatory response in the body and protect the skin.

- Include regular, gentle exercise to increase circulation to the skin.

- Try yoga or meditation to calm your nerves and help you sleep better (your skin always looks better when you're well rested).

- Use a gentle, natural cleanser, toner, and moisturizer daily.

- Wear sunscreen every day.

- Try using cold-pressed oils such as avocado oil and rose hip on your skin and hair to keep them nourished.

BALANCE YOUR BEAUTY TYPE AND MAINTAIN A LUSCIOUS COMPLEXION.

FIRE SKIN PRESCRIPTION

★ Try to cut back on carbonated drinks, caffeine, and super-salty or fried foods; they have little nutritional value and can aggravate your skin.

★ If your skin is prone to redness, rashes, and fiery red pimples, you might benefit from cutting back on spicy foods like chili, which can irritate the skin.

★ Wear sunscreen every day.

★ Add more fresh fruits and veggies to your diet; their antioxidant content is great for your skin.

★ Stress can wreak havoc on your skin; learn a form of meditation such as creative visualization to help you stay calm, cool, and collected.

★ Do regular exercise; swimming, yoga, weight training, and high-impact aerobics increase circulation to your skin.

★ Drink cooled herbal teas to detox your system and flush out your skin.

★ Treat any angry pimples with a drop of tea tree oil, which helps keep infections at bay.

★ Use a gentle, natural cleanser, toner, and moisturizer every day.

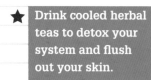

EARTH SKIN PRESCRIPTION

★ Try to cut back on high-fat and high-sugar foods; they create toxins in the body, which can show up on your skin.

★ Wear sunscreen every day.

★ A healthy digestive system means healthy skin; try to eat frequent smaller meals (big meals can stall digestion) full of whole grains, fruits, and veggies.

★ Add more fresh fruits and veggies to your diet to boost your antioxidant levels and keep your skin looking fabulous.

★ If you have slightly oily skin, don't dry it out. Use a lightweight moisturizer and keep your skin hydrated.

★ Do stimulating exercise like power walking, aerobics classes, weight training, or high-energy yoga; you'll increase your heart rate and circulation, which will help keep your skin clear and radiant.

★ Treat any deep zits with a compress of lavender or tea tree oil and warm water.

★ Do a morning body scrub with a brush or loofah before your shower to stimulate the micro-circulation in your skin and get your body detoxing. It will help you maintain smooth skin.

Clear skin strategies

Get this straight now.

Cosmetics can improve the texture, appearance, and now even the structure of the skin, but no cosmetic can replace the enduring benefits of inner health. Without the right nutrition and exercise, it's very hard to have great skin.

I know, you're thinking you know lots of girls with great skin who exist on a diet of junk food and whose exercise regimen consists of marathon DVD watching. But the fact is, those girls either have incredible genes or they'll see the results of their poor habits further down the track.

What you've inherited from your parents—your genes and possibly your Beauty Type—do factor heavily in how your skin looks and feels. It's important to learn how to work with the skin you're in and at the same time accept the gifts nature gave you. After all, you can't change your genes.

What you can do, however, is limit the havoc that pollution, sun damage, stress, poor nutrition, and lack of exercise may inflict on your skin. The good news is that with a little effort, these skin aggressors can largely be controlled.

One factor that's often left out of magazine articles about skin care is the impact your emotions have on your skin. You can be sure you'll get more breakouts when you're blue and there's not a girl on the planet who hasn't found Mount Vesuvius about to explode on her chin just before a hot date with a new guy. Long-term stress can translate into dryness, pimples, excessive oiliness, rashes, and even eczema and dermatitis.

The antidote to many of these emotionally induced skin complaints is to treat yourself and your skin to loads of rest and relaxation. Meditation, yoga, creative visualization, and anything else you can think of that makes you feel happy and content will all help improve the look and feel of your skin.

Where cosmetics may treat one aspect of your skin, a healthy diet, exercise, and the power of positive thought all play equally vital roles. You're about to get a breakdown of the basics—building blocks for year-round skin balance. Eliminate one of these fundamentals and the others have to work double-time to maintain good skin. By taking positive action and applying these simple principles, you'll create a feel-good routine that not only acts as a support system during stressful times but also unleashes the mega-beautifying powers of GirlForce.

Nothing ever works in isolation.

All the things you do to balance your skin—like eating right for your Beauty Type, getting tons of rest, regular exercise, yoga, and a consistent Beauty Type–balancing skin care routine—provides the building blocks to creating natural, confident beauty inside and out.

Cleansing inside

IT'S JUST AS IMPORTANT TO KEEP YOUR INTERNAL BODY CLEAN AND PROPERLY NOURISHED AS IT IS TO KEEP YOUR EXTERNAL BODY CLEAN AND PURE.

If your eating habits are less than perfect (like most of us), it's possible that any skin problems you're experiencing are a result of poor nutrition. If you're eating a lot of junk, your digestive system can become overburdened with food that's not properly digested and absorbed.

Okay, there are no magic solutions, but your skin will thank you if you follow an eating plan that's right for your Beauty Type. Here are some simple nutritional guidelines that can assist your digestive functioning and help you maintain year-round clear skin:

- ♥ Drink up to eight glasses of pure water each day.

- ♥ Avoid coffee, carbonated drinks, and alcohol; they leach the body of vitamins.

- ♥ Eat up to six servings a day of fresh fruits and veggies; the antioxidants they contain supply vital nutrients and vitamins to the skin.

- ♥ Eat three servings of fish each week; the omega-3 fatty acids in fish supply good fats to the skin, making it appear radiant and healthy.

- ♥ Cut down on processed foods and fried foods; they have low nutrient contents and may cause a variety of skin complaints.

- ♥ Eat seeds and nuts every day; they contain good fats and oils that protect your skin.

- ♥ Eat a low-sugar diet.

- ♥ Eat lots of foods that are high in vitamin C; it plays a key role in collagen production and the healthy functioning of the skin.

- ♥ Eat right for your Body Type (check out Chapter Five for more Beauty Type–balancing food suggestions).

- ♥ Contrary to the myths, there is no evidence that chocolate gives you zits (although white and milk chocolate have a high fat content).

 ## Air

A couple of times a week, make yourself fresh apple juice; the fruit acids and antioxidants A, B, C, and E will help cleanse and detox your skin.

 ## *Fire*

A couple of times a week, make yourself watermelon juice; the alkaline minerals in the melon help rid the body of acids and help clarify your skin.

Earth

A couple of times a week, make yourself pear juice; the cleansing minerals in pears help promote effective digestion and elimination, which also help detox and tone your skin.

Cleansing with juice

Exercise

IS ABSOLUTELY KEY TO BALANCING YOUR MIND, BODY, AND SPIRIT.

Stress blocks the immune system, hampers digestion, and stimulates the adrenal glands—one big factor in the acne cycle. So when stress is "worked out" of your body through exercise, your internal systems perform their duties more efficiently.

Exercise also helps clarify and tone the complexion, however, the benefits go way beyond the skin. Here are a few reasons why you should think about incorporating Beauty Type–balancing exercise into your daily routine:

- It raises the metabolic rate so cells burn oxygen more efficiently; this increases the rate at which energy is released from food, in turn releasing more nutrients to the skin.

- It promotes better elimination, which helps to keep the skin clear.

- It improves the condition of the heart, lungs, and circulation, promoting micro-circulation in the skin.

- It boosts the production of "happy" chemicals and helps prevent depression, stress, and fatigue.

- It strengthens the muscles, bones, and joints.

- And last but not least, it's fun!

Clear-Skin Exercise Prescription

- Walk 4 times a week for 30 minutes, breaking a light sweat. Air girls can stroll, Fire girls can walk briskly, and Earth girls should power walk.

- Drink two glasses of water after your walks and wash your body and face in the shower with a gentle body wash (don't use soap because it can be too drying).

CHECK OUT CHAPTER FIVE FOR INFO ON WHICH EXERCISE PLANS WILL BALANCE YOUR PARTICULAR BEAUTY TYPE.

Stress management strategies

STRESS TAKES A TOLL ON THE BODY AND SOUL.

But what is stress and what can you do about it? Stress is really the way you react internally to something that happens externally. In other words, it's your reaction to life. Stressors such as your environment, lack of sleep, not enough exercise, poor nutrition, and negative thoughts can affect us on a daily basis.

The best way to get a handle on stress is to become aware of your reactions to it. Exams are stressful; you get anxious, worry about the outcome, forget to eat, lose sleep, etc. What if you could control these reactions? Wouldn't you feel amazing if an exam day was just like any other day? The good news is, you can control your reactions to stress, and here's how:

- Practice regular affirmations. (See page 46!)
- Start a journal and write down all the things that stress you out and why.
- Learn to develop a "witness consciousness" where you can witness yourself being stressed out and laugh at your reactions.
- Do regular exercise. It brings down stress levels and curbs adrenaline output so you feel less anxious.
- Do regular meditation. It calms the mind and helps you control your reactions to stress.
- Do regular yoga. It helps balance the mind, body, and spirit and brings down anxiety levels.

Clear skin

STRESS SOLUTION

Proper breathing is not only essential to well-being, it also helps create a flawless complexion by reducing stress. Most of us use only a third of our lung capacity and as a result are prone to lethargy, depression, and poor digestion.

One simple exercise is to lie on your back with your arms by your side and the palms of your hands facing upward. Breathe in through your nostrils and concentrate the full force of your breath into your lower abdomen. Watch the abdomen rise as you inhale and slowly deflate as you exhale. Continue to breathe through the nostrils and repeat for 2 rounds of 10 breaths.

Affirmations are an effective tool to help you get what you want in life.

They offer a way to train your mind to think of positive outcomes. Whether you're after a fit bod, improved relationships with your friends and family, or clearer skin, affirmations can help you get there.

Okay, they won't deliver results overnight, but they will help you put away negative thoughts and tune you into new, bright possibilities. Repeat your own or any of the following affirmations to yourself in front of the mirror and see how you feel after a couple of weeks of practicing them. You might feel kinda goofy at first, but keep going—these affirmations will give you confidence and boost GirlForce:

- I AM PERFECT JUST THE WAY I AM.
- MY SKIN IS GETTING CLEARER AND HEALTHIER EVERY DAY.
- I LOVE MYSELF.
- I AM AT PEACE WITH MYSELF.
- EVERY DAY I EXPERIENCE THE CONFIDENCE-BOOSTING POWERS OF GIRLFORCE SURGE THROUGH ME.
- EVERYTHING ABOUT ME IS A WONDROUS EXPRESSION OF NATURE.
- I AM A CELEBRATION OF DIVINE LOVE.
- I AM EMPOWERED TO EXERCISE EVERY DAY.
- I AM BEAUTIFUL BECAUSE I AM UNIQUE.
- I FLOW WITH EVERYTHING IN MY LIFE LIKE A RIVER.

Power

of positive thought

Get ready to turn up the volume on your shine-o-meter.

The two main factors that determine the success of any skin care plan are patience and persistence.
The daily ritual of cleansing, toning, and moisturizing, followed by sun protection, are vital to the long-term health and balance of your skin.

Regular masks (turn to Chapter Four to discover some yummy natural Ayurvedic skin treatments) and exfoliation are also important steps in maintaining good skin.

If you want a healthy, luscious, glowing complexion, don't skip any of these steps and make sure you pamper your skin every day.

Discover

SKIN RADIANCE

Step **1**

CLEANSE

Most cosmetics companies will tell you to cleanse twice a day. Personally, I think it's okay to use a cleanser once a day as long as you rinse off all your make-up and get rid of any dirt and grease. For that reason I like to shower at night with a foaming cleanser that removes all traces of make-up and leaves my skin fresh but not stripped bare.

To refresh and clean the skin in the morning I recommend washing your face with warm or warm-to-cool water with a washcloth and a few drops of either lavender or chamomile essential oil dropped onto it. (The water will clean your skin and the essential oils will stimulate the senses and get rid of any grease or bacteria on the skin.)

For a bright and clear complexion, your goal with cleansing is not just to get rid of dirt, make-up, and oil; it's also to seal in the moisture that's already on the skin and prepare it to accept the ingredients in your moisturizer. Choose a lightweight and gentle rinse-off foaming cleanser that leaves the skin fresh and clean without drying it out. If you prefer a cream cleanser, go for a light and gentle product that won't leave a greasy film on the skin. Baby oil, olive oil, and soap will all remove make-up, but when it comes to cleansers, there's no doubt that skin care companies make the most efficient ones.

Step 2

TONE

Toning is one great way to help balance your skin and prevent pimples, especially if you use an essential oil toner. The antiviral, antibacterial, and anti-inflammatory properties in essential oils will not only rid the skin of any germs, they will also reduce the risk of irritation and balance the oil in the skin, helping to prevent further outbreaks. You can make one up yourself with 4 tablespoons of purified water and 10 drops of rose essential oil. Shake it up to disperse the oil and spray on your face. Rose balances every skin type.

Step 3

MOISTURIZE

Clear skin is hard to achieve without an effective moisturizer. The best ones plump up the skin with molecules that bind water to the cells and also deliver ingredients that protect the skin from sun damage, pollution, and stress. In other words, they deposit vitamins to help slow down free-radical damage. Try to find products that have a lot of essential oils listed at the top of the label and also go for products that are enhanced with vitamins such as A, C, and E or green tea.

As a rule of thumb, lotions are lightweight and good for oilier skin types (like Earth skins and some acne-prone Fire skins), and creams are more beneficial for drier skin types (such as Air skins). It's all about trial and error, but look for products that contain calming and soothing botanical ingredients (such as essential oils) and a sunscreen of at least SPF 15.

One of the most effective ways to say good-bye to dry, dull, lifeless skin is to exfoliate regularly. There are two main ways to rid the skin of dead cells: you can use a chemical exfoliator (such as glycolic, lactic, or salicylic acid) or you can use a mechanical or physical exfoliator (such as sugar, salt, or oatmeal, or a product with synthetic granules).

A great DIY scrub is a mixture of a handful of rolled oats, a tablespoon of honey, and 4 teaspoons of milk. The milk contains lactic acid, which helps refine the texture of the skin, and the oats slough away dead cells. Simply massage the mixture over your skin and rinse away with warm water.

Voilà, no more flaky skin.

Once a week it's a good idea to treat your skin to a luscious mask. Masks help draw out impurities, reduce any inflammation (that may be caused by deep pimples), and banish blackheads and oil.

Most health food stores carry a range of dry clays (they come in red, green, and white powders) and they make excellent masks. Depending on the porousness of the clays, you add water until it becomes a paste by stirring in the water with a spoon. Once you have a paste-like consistency, add five drops of an essential oil. Either choose an oil according to your Beauty Type (see below) or select one according to your skin condition: geranium and sandalwood are good for dry skin; rosemary and lemon are good for oily skin; sage and tea tree will help treat zits; and rose and chamomile are good for sensitive skins.

It's not a big deal for you right now (apart from getting sunburned), but it's really important to understand that, no matter what your skin color, sun damage is the main reason your skin ages. If you don't want wrinkles, dryness, and pigmented skin later in life, you'll have to take steps NOW to protect yourself. Also, you need to know that according to the Centers for Disease Control and Prevention, skin cancer is the most common form of cancer in the United States and 90 percent of all skin cancers are due to sun damage. Protect your skin's future by wearing sunscreen daily.

Step **4**

EXFOLIATE

Step **5**

TREAT

Step **6**

PROTECT

DAILY SKIN RITUALS
for everyone

A.M. ROUTINE

1. Fill your bathroom sink with warm water and add five drops of a Beauty Type–specific essential oil (see page 57). Dunk a facecloth into the water and wring it out. Pat the cloth over your face for a minute, softening the pores on your skin, and breathe in the soothing and harmonizing aroma of the essential oil. Allow the skin to dry.

2. Spritz your face with a toner made from 4 tablespoons of spring water and ten drops of geranium or rose essential oil in a spray.

3. Apply your daily moisturizer with built-in sunscreen.

4. Apply make-up.

P.M. ROUTINE

1. Use a foaming or cream cleanser to remove any make-up, grime, or grease.

2. Spritz your face with a toner made from 4 tablespoons of spring water and ten drops of chamomile essential oil in a spray.

3. Apply a night moisturizer or an essential oil (see page 56) and cold-pressed oil (like wheat germ or rose hip) to nourish your skin.

Once a week

- Apply a moisturizing and calming mask.
- Gently exfoliate your skin.

Essential oils & you

Essential oils are powerful healing plant, fruit, and flower extracts. They have antibacterial, antiviral, and anti-inflammatory properties and have been used for centuries to help de-stress the mind, cleanse the body, and purify the spirit through an amazing combo of touch and smell. Essential oils are also one of your most powerful skin care weapons. They help fend off zits, banish grease, reduce redness, and tone and balance your complexion.

Added to a cream, massaged into your skin, dropped onto a cloth, or sprayed onto your body, they not only cleanse and harmonize your skin, they also lift your emotions and make you feel awesome.

Use the following essential oils to balance and harmonize each Beauty Type's complexion.

AIR:
bergamot, chamomile, geranium, neroli, patchouli, rose, sandalwood

FIRE:
jasmine, lavender, lemon, lemongrass, peppermint, sandalwood, tea tree

EARTH:
bergamot, cinnamon, grapefruit, lavender, lemon, patchouli, sunflower

One of the main aims of aromatherapy is to discover different ways of getting essential oils to penetrate the body. When they enter the bloodstream, they act on the vital systems (such as the central nervous and the lymphatic systems) as well as muscles, tissues, the brain, and the skin. And by boosting the body's own defense mechanisms via touch and smell, aromatherapy helps restore balance and vitality.

One great thing about adding essential oils to your daily beauty routine is that they're easy to get your hands on (and they're not that expensive). Most health food stores carry a range of good oils, and because they come in little bottles—which are easy to transport— you can even throw them into your schoolbag for a quick beauty booster.

If you use them as part of your daily self-pampering and beauty rituals, you'll discover a new path to beauty and confidence.

Air GIRL

Take a washcloth (and a small plastic bag to stow your cloth once it's damp) to school along with a bottle of chamomile essential oil. When you feel stressed and tired, add a couple of drops of chamomile to the warm cloth and place it over your face and the back of your neck. The warm water will help hydrate your skin and the chamomile will calm your nerves.

Make a great nourishing day and night skin booster with a blend of five drops of geranium, three drops of chamomile, and three drops of bergamot essential oil in a bottle filled with 4 teaspoons of olive oil.

Fire GIRL

Make up a small bottle with 4 teaspoons of coconut oil and add three drops of lavender, two drops of patchouli, and three drops of sandalwood. Use it as a body moisturizer and rub into your legs, arms, and torso each morning. The coconut will hydrate and soften your skin and the lavender and sandalwood will keep your emotions cool, calm, and collected.

For a cooling and soothing moisturizer, add two drops of rosemary, three drops of lavender, and two drops of lemon essential oil into 4 teaspoons of sweet almond oil and apply morning and night.

Earth GIRL

Make a pick-me-up spritz of 4 tablespoons purified water, five drops of bergamot, and three drops of cinnamon. Spritz from head to toe to keep your skin clean and hydrated and your emotions balanced and happy.

For a refreshing and stimulating day and night moisturizing treatment, add four drops of lavender, two drops of bergamot, and two drops of clary sage essential oil to 4 teaspoons of sunflower oil.

(Go for an organic sunflower oil from the health food store, not the mass-produced sunflower oil from the supermarket.)

Daily essential oil beauty tools

DIFFERENT SKIN TYPES

Sensitive skin

Sensitive skin isn't always simply a matter of dryness or redness. Technically, skin sensitivity includes eczema, allergies, rashes, and dermatitis.

If a doctor or dermatologist has diagnosed any of these conditions, you'll hopefully be informed about what chemicals and lifestyle factors to avoid and how to treat your skin.

Fire Beauty Types are most susceptible to extreme skin sensitivity, although it can happen to anyone who becomes "sensitized" to a particular chemical or stress. However, if you find your skin burns or tingles after using cosmetics or it feels itchy, red, and dry a lot of the time, you'll benefit from the following guidelines:

💜 Avoid extreme temperature changes (especially if you're a Fire girl).

💜 Avoid too much sun exposure (again, especially if you're Fire).

💜 Avoid too many spicy foods (you guessed it, especially if you're Fire).

💜 Opt for natural skin care that doesn't contain harsh detergents.

💜 Don't exfoliate your skin too rigorously.

💜 Try a new sunscreen. Some sunscreens contain chemicals that can cause your skin to become irritated and sensitive.

💜 Avoid cosmetics with strong fragrances. Perfumes added to skin products are the most common irritants.

💜 Don't use soap on your skin. It can disrupt the lipid barrier in the skin and cause dryness and sensitivity.

Dry skin

Sun- or windburn, air-conditioning, central heating, too many hot showers, and stress all can cause dry, flaky skin. Air Types are most susceptible to dry skin, but if you're out of balance, dry patches can appear anywhere on your body.

To prevent dry skin, try these easy remedies:

* Use a daily moisturizer on your face and body.
* Avoid prolonged wind exposure.
* Don't get sunburned.
* Do a weekly exfoliation treatment.
* Add oily fish such as salmon, mackerel, and sardines to your diet.
* Add olive or flaxseed oil to your salads.
* Avoid long, hot showers.
* Get loads of R&R.

Normal/combination skin

Many of you have normal/ combination skin that isn't overly sensitive or excessively dry or severely acne-prone.

You may find you have an oily T-zone and drier cheeks and temples. Or you may get the odd blackhead or zit around your period or exams. Changes in your environment, the seasons, hormones, and stress can all show up on your skin; however, you probably notice that your skin returns to balance fairly quickly. Even if you don't "suffer" from any serious skin problem, you still need to maintain your daily rituals and look after your skin.

When you look after your skin daily, it *glows* with good health.

Of all the skin problems, the treatment of acne is probably the most controversial. While the exact causes are not completely understood, most dermatologists believe genetic and hormonal factors are the major contributors. Other factors could include stress, lack of exercise, and an inadequate diet. And according to Ayurveda, any Beauty Type can get zits during puberty and may experience more severe acne when they're out of balance.

Arrgh! I've got zits

Mostly, zits disappear in your 20s (good news, huh?), but about 10 percent of people continue to get acne into their 30s and 40s. By now you've probably discovered that your hormones are wreaking havoc with your skin. Your menstrual cycle can contribute to the appearance of blemishes on your face, chest, and back.

Acne and oily skin develop from the increased production of sebum, secreted by the sebaceous glands. It's sticky and blocks pores and creates blackheads and whiteheads. Sebum is also irritating to the skin and produces red lumps. It's a paradise for bacteria and can lead to little infections that show up as sore, angry zits.

It takes about five weeks for a pimple to develop and disappear, and because most treatments aim to prevent the formation of new zits, it can take more than a month for a new treatment to produce any noticeable results. (This is where patience comes in!)

Some dermatologists advise that the skin needs to be cleared of oil before it can normalize, but there's another school of thought that asserts that oily and acne-prone skin should be treated slowly and gently with nonaggressive, non-drying treatments that don't disturb the pores or pustules. Many believe that stripping the skin of its oil only makes it work harder to replace the oil that's been lost, resulting in more oil and sometimes more zits.

In my experience, one of the best treatments for acne is essential oil. A dab of tea tree or lavender oil on an angry zit can prevent infection and speed the healing process. Daily cleansing with five drops of lavender oil in a sink full of water will also help prevent the spread of bacteria on your skin and help stop new zits in their tracks. A mixture of 4 tablespoons of sweet almond oil with five drops of chamomile, four drops of geranium, two drops of lavender, and two drops of rosemary will help calm, tone, and disinfect your skin.

Today, doctors can treat severe acne with antibiotics, lasers, and antibiotic gels and creams. If you have more than a few zits on your face, neck, back, and chest, you should seek the advice of a doctor.

What's so bad about squeezing zits? Most beauty consultants and doctors agree that squeezing zits is the single biggest beauty mistake you can make. It spreads infection, makes the pimples sore and irritated, and can lead to scarring. What happens when you pop a pimple is that you generally rupture the oil gland, miss the core, and push the infection into other parts of the pore. Then the pimple becomes reinfected, inflamed, and bruised.

Okay, lecture over. Sometimes the zit is so unsightly it needs to be squeezed. If you can afford it, it's best to let a trained dermatologist do it, but failing that, what's a girl to do when a big zit raises its ugly head? Frankly, most girls are going to squeeze it! If you are going to squeeze a pimple, this is the way facialists do it:

1. Fill the sink with warm water and five drops of lavender essential oil. Dunk a washcloth in the water.

2. Wring out the washcloth and press it against the zit. The heat will soften the pustule and the lavender will help disinfect the area.

3. Get two tissues and wrap them around your fingertips. Press gently on the pimple, trying to get underneath the infected part. Hopefully the goop will come out with the core. If the pimple is a nasty, deep one, you might have to sterilize a needle (put it into a flame for a couple of seconds) and prick the head.

4. After you've squeezed, dab on some tea tree or lavender oil and leave it to dry.

5. If you have to cover it up, wait until it has dried and started to form a scab, then put on a tiny dot of concealer.

DISCOVER THE SECRETS OF SAFE

squeezing

sun
protection

FOR EVERYONE

So you haven't got wrinkles—yet.

Did you know that almost all of what we see as aging skin—that is, wrinkles, blotchiness, dryness, redness, and pigmentation—are the result of sun damage? Wrinkles are a normal fact of life, and as you age you'll learn how to live with them, but skin cancer is the most serious side effect of sun damage and it affects hundreds of thousands of people every year.

Your best defense against sun damage and skin cancer is to stay out of the sun—which is not practical or much fun. So your next best option is to cover up. When you go outside, wear sunscreen—during summer and winter. You'll also need to apply your sunscreen every two hours if you're in direct sunlight. If you're spending a lot of time outside, hanging at the beach, or playing a sport, try to wear protective clothing like a hat, sunglasses, a long-sleeved shirt, and a sarong.

Think of this: Your skin is an active organ weighing about six and a half pounds. Each inch contains about three feet of blood vessels, twenty-five nerve endings, one hundred sweat glands, and over three million cells. The skin's primary function is to protect. It forms a living, breathing suit of armor that keeps our organs and bones safe and defends us against environmental invaders.

This biological super-guardian also eliminates waste (perspiration), manufactures vitamins, and, with its thousands of sensory nerve endings, warns of danger and gives us the pleasure of touch. It can also absorb both harmful and beneficial substances into its deepest layers, which is why it can be affected by the application of cosmetics and essential oils.

CHAPTER THREE

Make-up lesson

A glam, professional look is just steps away

Make-up that looks like it was applied by a pro isn't nearly as hard as you'd think. All it takes is a little practice, a dash of confidence, and the right tools and techniques for your Beauty Type. And with these simple-to-master tricks of the trade, you'll be able to transform yourself from girl-next-door into a GirlForce goddess in no time.

There are times when a bare face is not only appropriate (say for gym class), it's positively liberating.

One of the best ways to celebrate the real YOU is to stand in front of a mirror with no make-up on and simply look at yourself. The challenge is to look at your reflection and not say anything negative about the face staring back at you. One of the key aspects of GirlForce is learning to love yourself and your unique beauty—just the way you are. That means liking yourself on a bad hair day or with a face full of zits.

When you can do that, you are one *powerful chick!* A bare face can be an empowered face.

THAT SAID, there are times when it's not only appropriate to wear make-up (to your school dance, for example), it's a blast! One of the best parts of being a girl is that we get to dress up. Women have been applying make-up since the beginning of time. The ritual of putting on make-up is one of the most sensuous, private, and exhilarating things a girl can do for herself. The mere act of transforming yourself from a nude face to a made-up babe is magic.

As a beauty editor

I am biased, but

I love make-up.

I love the feeling of the pigments sweeping over my skin. I love the smell of fresh lipstick in a tube and I adore the way I look when my face is properly made up.

In my role as a beauty editor for glossy magazines, I have had access to some of the world's best make-up artists and hairdressers. Their top tips and hints are all here in these pages, and they work for everyone no matter your face shape or individual features. The best tip I can give you is to have fun and experiment, and eventually you'll perfect the techniques like a pro!

And I want to let you in on a secret while I'm at it: there's hardly a woman on the planet who does not look better with a little make-up. And those chicks with great skin who can wear next to nothing on their faces? Even they generally need a little help to even out their complexions—usually a sheer foundation.

Applying make-up well is both an art and a science. The art is in applying the right colors and textures to enhance your looks, and the science is all about the right tools and techniques. Thanks to modern technology, pretty much anyone can get their hands on the right products and tools, so making-up is easy to do—when you know how.

You're going to learn how to apply make-up like a pro. You'll discover all the tricks of the trade to play up your assets and be Beauty Type beautiful—

like how to bring out the sparkle of Air Type eyes or make the most of Fire-girl freckles or contour a rounded Earth Type face. You're also going to discover that make-up can do much more for you than make you look good. It can make you feel good, too. Check out the section on mood make-up—you'll never think the same way about making up your face again!

So next time you feel down in the dumps because your skin is a mess or your features are less than perfect, cheer up. With the following tools and techniques, you'll be able to face the world with a full tank of confidence.

Be Beauty Type beautiful and discover how to make the most of your features.

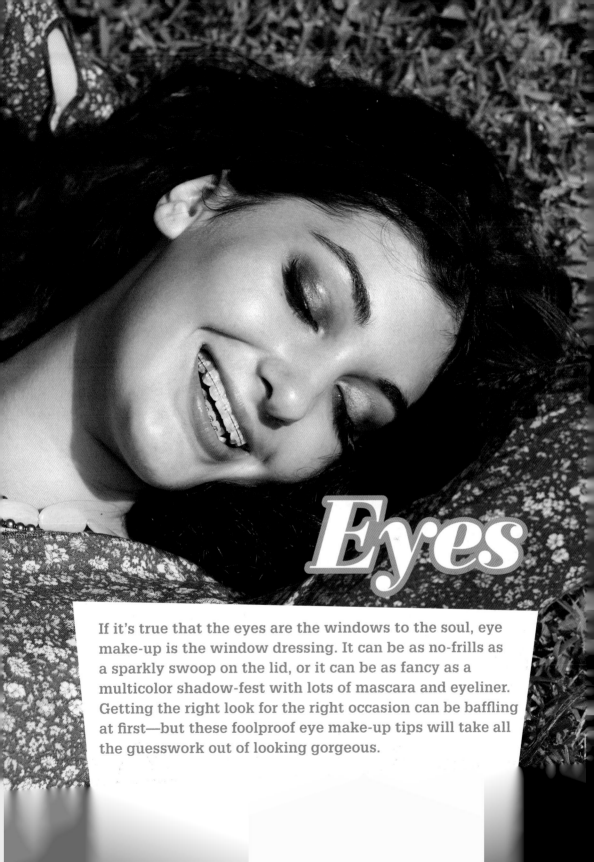

Eyes

If it's true that the eyes are the windows to the soul, eye make-up is the window dressing. It can be as no-frills as a sparkly swoop on the lid, or it can be as fancy as a multicolor shadow-fest with lots of mascara and eyeliner. Getting the right look for the right occasion can be baffling at first—but these foolproof eye make-up tips will take all the guesswork out of looking gorgeous.

AIR eyes

For small eyes, make them pop:

★ Line the inner eye with a white or light blue pencil to open them up.

★ Avoid dark colors on the lids; it closes the eyes.

★ Use a medium-shade shadow for the crease and use a darker color on the outer edge of the lids.

★ Curl lashes and use a thickening mascara.

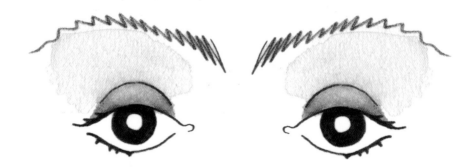

For close-set eyes, create an illusion of space:

★ Keep the emphasis on the outer corners; use a dark pencil to rim the eyes, taking the liner to the middle of the upper and lower lids.

★ Use a light eye shadow on the inner corners of the eyes.

FIRE *eyes*

Almond-shaped eyes

**are the easiest to make up.
Just about anything goes:**

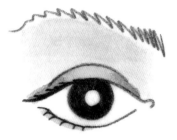 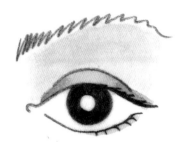

★ For daytime, just smudge a little of your favorite shimmer over the entire lid and apply a coat of mascara.

★ For night, rim the upper and lower lids in a dark liner and smudge some dark eye shadow into the outer corners.

 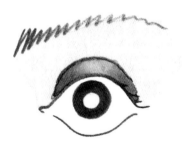

For round eyes, **the aim is to elongate:**

★ Line the upper lid with a dark pencil and extend the line just past the outer corner.

★ Smudge a little dark eye shadow into the outer and inner corners of the upper lids.

★ Apply a thickening and lengthening mascara to the lashes (especially on the outer corners of the eyes).

EARTH *eyes*

For wide-set eyes:

bring them together:

★ Focus attention on the inner corners of the eyes; line the upper and lower lids with a dark pencil.

★ Avoid light colors on the inside corners of the eyes.

★ Smudge a medium-shade eye shadow over the upper eyelid and blend it toward the outer corners of the eyes.

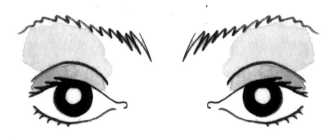

If your eyes are hooded or deep-set:

you need to:

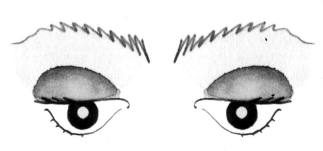

★ Define the lash line by lining around the upper and lower lids with a dark pencil.

★ Apply a medium-shade eye shadow onto the eyelid and blend it into the socket to create a contour in the crease of the eye; this will open the eyes.

★ Avoid light shades on the fleshy part of the lid.

If you have Asian eyes, check out these extra tips for your eye shape. It might help to combine these points with your Beauty Type tips!

For Asian eyes,

add some allure:

★ Accentuate the eyes by drawing a thick pencil line from the middle of the upper lash to the outer corners and along the bottom lids.

★ Use dark colors on the upper lid to give definition, but don't use dark shades to try to create a crease; it will look unnatural.

★ Use a light, shimmering shade, not white, on the eyelids to the brow bone (white will make the eyes too heavy lidded).

★ Curl lashes and use a curling and lengthening mascara.

Lips

Let's admit it: life would be drastically dull without lip color.

Whether it's gooey and glossy, silky smooth and matte, velvety and rich, or totally transparent and shimmering like the stars, it's completely addictive. A change from sheer to opaque can transform your look from pouty princess to sexy vamp. Pump up the volume on your kisser with these lip-smackingly simple techniques.

Air lips

For thin lips:

- Trace the outline of the entire mouth with a neutral-toned lip pencil and blend it into the lips so it doesn't look like a hard line around the mouth.

- Apply lipstick and go for a mid-tone (not too light and not too dark).

- Dot a touch of lip gloss into the center of the top and bottom lips.

If lips are uneven:

- Use a nude-shade lip pencil to "draw" a more even shape and blend the liner into the lips with your fingertips.

- Create balance to a noticeably fuller top or bottom lip by using a natural-toned lipstick all over the mouth and dabbing gloss on the thinner lip.

FIRE LIPS

To make medium-shaped lips

look slightly fuller:

- Use a berry or warm-toned brown lipstick or gloss (lighter colors will make your lips look thinner).
- Use shimmer or gloss on the lower lip to make the lips look poutier.

EARTH LIPS For full lips:

- To play them down, use a light-colored lipstick or a color gloss.
- To play them up, use a deep shade and dab gloss onto the center of the bottom lip.
- If you want a darker look for night, dab a mid-shade such as berry into the center of the top and bottom lips and blend outward with your fingers.

For bow-shaped lips:

- Apply a neutral shade to "soften" the points of the lips.

- Add a dab of gloss to the center of the bottom lip.

- To extend the look of the mouth, use a dark-shade lip liner and draw only along the outer edges of the lips; don't line the whole mouth. Blend the line with your fingertips to soften it.

Foundation

You don't need full-on paint to make your complexion look flawless. The right foundation for your skin tone and texture will not only conceal any blemishes, it will make you look like you were born to be

fabulous.

Air

- Air skin is prone to dryness, so go for liquid formulas that are boosted with moisturizers.

- If you have a smattering of freckles and want to show them off, use a tinted moisturizer.

- If you want to soften dark freckles or have dark under-eye circles, dab on a light liquid concealer before you apply your foundation.

- If you have dark brown, olive, or bluish undertones in your skin, go for cool-toned foundations that have blue and cool brown pigments; avoid yellow- or pink-toned foundations and concealers.

Fire

🌼 Fire skin can be prone to breakouts, so opt for oil-free foundations that won't clog your pores. Try a light liquid or a sheer tinted moisturizer formula.

🌼 If your skin has red undertones (like many Fire chicks), go for a foundation that has rose pigments to complement the natural flush of your skin.

🌼 Avoid yellow- and blue-toned foundations and concealers.

🌼 Dab a drop of lavender essential oil on any zits and apply a medicated concealer under foundation.

🌼 *Freckles are cool!* To show 'em off, use a liquid foundation mixed with your moisturizer to create a sheer cover.

Earth

🌼 Earth skin can be a bit greasy, especially on the T-zone. Go for a foundation that's formulated to compensate for oiliness on the T-zone and dryness on the cheeks and forehead. Stick and compact foundations are great if you have combination skin, or use a matte foundation if your skin is extra oily.

🌼 If you have under-eye bags, use a light liquid concealer mixed with your moisturizer under the eyes and blend into the skin before applying foundation.

🌼 Earth girls are often pale for their race. Go for foundations that are sheer and lightweight as thick, creamy pigmented foundations can look chalky on paler, flatter skin tones.

🌼 If your skin has yellow undertones, go for yellow-based foundations.

FOUNDATION APPLICATION

Pick the right shade

The best way to pick a foundation that's color-correct for your skin tone is to go to a beauty counter and draw streaks of color on your jawline and look in a mirror. The exact shade for your skin will literally disappear before your eyes.

Totally addicted to base

Before you apply your foundation, start by moisturizing your skin and let it sink in for a minute. Dot foundation onto your cheeks, forehead, nose, and chin. With your fingers or a sponge, blend outward toward the sides of your face with small strokes, patting gently around the eyes. At the hairline and jawline, it should fade to nothing. If you like a minimal foundation look, just apply the foundation to your T-zone—it will even out your complexion without making you look made up.

Ready, set, go!

Dip a large fluffy brush into a pot of translucent loose powder. Flick the excess powder into the pot, then dust it lightly over the face; this will set the foundation. Girls with dry skin can skip this step.

Tricks OF THE TRADE

FOUNDATION HINTS:

★ For an even application of liquid foundation, pour it into the palm of your hand to warm it before you apply it (the heat of your hands makes it easier to blend).

★ With a small brush, dot foundation over blemishes and blend it with your fingertips.

★ Soak up any excess by pressing a tissue gently onto your face. You'll also notice this catches a little excess oil, too.

★ As a rule of thumb, dry skin types should go for moisturizing foundations such as creams and liquids. Oily skin types should look for oil-free or matte foundations; combination skin types should go for products that both hydrate and absorb, to compensate for dryness on the cheeks and reduce oil on the T-zone. Finally, normal skin types can use any foundation—liquid, cream, powder, or stick. Don't be afraid to experiment and find what works best for you.

AIR

If you have a long face, a very small face, or a triangular face, the best place to apply blush is the apples of your cheeks. A little color on the apples will bring brightness to your face and enhance your sparkly eyes. To find them, make an exaggerated smile; the fleshy part of the cheek that lifts up is the apple. In circular motions, apply a light dusting of a powder blush or a cream.

FIRE

If you have a round, oval, or heart-shaped face, the best place to apply blush is also the apples of the cheeks. To find them, make an exaggerated smile; the fleshy part of the cheek that lifts up is the apple. In circular motions, apply a light dusting of a powder blush or a cream. A flush of pretty pink, orange, or berry on the cheeks will give your skin a healthy glow and complement the natural pigment in your lips.

EARTH

If you have a square or round face, the best way to bring out your cheekbones and create the illusion that you have Cate Blanchett's bone structure is to contour with your blush. Start by pulling your hair away from your face. Draw an imaginary line from the outside corner of your mouth to the middle of your ear where it joins the side of your face—that's the underside of your cheekbones. Using a fat brush, sweep color along the underside of the cheekbones from the ears toward the middle of the face. Technically, your blush should stop directly under your pupils under the cheekbones. If you prefer to use a cream blush, make sure you blend the color with your fingertips or it will look like you've swiped something sticky onto your cheeks.

Blush and contour

Depending on the shape of your face, there are two places to apply blush—on the apple of your cheeks or along the underside of your cheekbones.

EYEBROWS

The eyebrows are an important part of your face because they show expression and reveal emotion. Everyone's eyebrows are unique—sometimes they're arched and definite like a Fire babe's, fine like an Air girl's, and sometimes they're bushy like an Earth angel's.

The best way to shape your eyebrows is to use your natural arch as a guide and very carefully tweeze away stray hairs. Be sure to stop and take stock after every few hairs to avoid tweezing too much. An eyebrow pencil is a great addition to any kit because it helps give your brows shape and definition.

One of the best ways to shape your eyebrows is to square off the inner brow near the nose by filling in any little gaps with a pencil. Create a graceful arch in the middle by feathering the pencil to a point at the top of the middle of the brow. Taper the brow line to a point at the edge near the side of your face. Make sure you use a pencil that's the exact tone of your eyebrows—if you use a shade that's too dark you'll look overly made-up.

Make-up must-haves

1. Moisturizer

2. Concealer

(liquid if you have
dry skin and stick
if you have normal
or combination skin)

3. Foundation

(liquid if you have dry
skin, matte formulas
if you have oily skin,
and compact or stick
if you have normal
or combination)

4. Loose powder

(great if you want
to cut back shine)

5. Cream or
powder blush

(creams and gels are
fun and easy to apply,
especially if you have
dry skin)

6. Eyeliner

(brown, black, or blue
are handy additions
to your kit)

7. Eye shadow

(select colors according to your Beauty Type; a shimmering gold or silver looks good on most skin tones; and keep a black, brown, or charcoal in your kit for contouring)

8. Mascara

(black is an essential; blue and brown are great for daytime looks)

9. Lip pencil

(a nude lip pencil is a great tool for making up your mouth, especially if you have unevenly shaped lips or you want your lipstick to last)

10. Shimmer stick

(for summer, swipe it over the cheeks, lips, and temples to get a sun-kissed glow)

11. Lip gloss

(a clear lip gloss, perhaps with a little shimmer, will change the look of any lipstick and can be worn alone every day)

Most girls would sooner give up a boyfriend than ditch their fave lip gloss. So no one is going to suggest you go cold turkey and skip make-up on the weekend. In fact, the weekend is the perfect time to live a little and have fun with make-up. GO ON, EXPERIMENT. You don't have to paint it on. It can be sweet, sheer, and subtle, but a stroke of mascara and dab of color on your cheeks and lips can transform you from girl-next-door into red-carpet cool—even if it's just for a trip to the mall.

Follow these easy steps and *voilà,* you're ready to walk out the door feeling on top of the world!

Step 1 Moisturize.

Step 2 Dab some concealer over any zits or blemishes and blend with your fingertips.

Step 3 Apply a little shimmering bronzer or blush to your cheeks.

Step 4 Stroke on mascara, but just to the ends of the lashes so you don't look overly done. Try a colored mascara for a striking change.

Step 5 Dab on lip gloss.

Step 6 Spritz on some perfume to give you sassy style.

Tricks OF THE TRADE

★ To make your eyes look whiter, apply a light dusting of bronzing powder over your eyes, cheeks, and temples.

★ If your eyes look a little puffy, soak two chamomile tea bags in cool water and lie down for 20 minutes with them over your eyes (the chamomile will help drain any excess fluid in your skin).

★ Cover blemishes with a concealer that matches your skin tone.

★ Use an eyelash curler before applying your mascara to really "open" your eyes and give them that va-va-voom look.

★ A swipe of a pale shimmering cream in a shade such as beige, brown, cream, or apricot, depending on your skin color, will give your eyes instant glamour. You only need a dash of lip gloss and a sweep of mascara to look polished, yet not made-up.

Wanna make a statement?

Never underestimate the power of sultry make-up applied to perfection. Nighttime make-up does not have to look overdone. The clever handling of color and texture can look totally glam and sexy without making you look like a clown. Here's how to go from natural to knockout and shake up your image with confidence and style.

NIGHTTIME knockout

knockout

Step 1   Moisturize.

Step 2   Dab some concealer over any zits or blemishes and blend with your fingertips.

Step 3   Apply your foundation.

Step 4   If you want a matte look, dust a light veil of powder over your T-zone.

Step 5   Use either a cream or a powder blush and sweep color onto your cheeks to define or create a gorgeous shape. Choose a shimmering blush to give you a summery glow.

Step 6   Select your favorite color eye shadow (pale blue or pink are great if you're an Air girl, white or lime are fab if you're Fire, and caramel or orange are terrific if you're Earth). Use a brush to cover the entire lid up to the brow in a sheer swoop of color. (If you need to use a contouring shade to give your eyes depth and definition, use a hint of smoky gray at the outer corners of your eyes and follow the instructions for your eye shape, as on pages 80 through 83).

Step 7   Use a black, gray, or dark blue eyeliner and rim the eyes according to your eye shape. Make a little smudge with your fingertips to the outside corners of the eyes for that sultry nighttime look.

Step 8   Use a mascara that's going to pick up every lash and double its size and make your eyelashes look really lush.

Step 9   Groom your eyebrows with an eyebrow pencil by filling in any little gaps and giving your eyebrows shape and definition.

Step 10   Find a super-shimmery lip gloss—go for either a pale light-reflecting shade for an oh-so-sassy smile, or a deep cherry for a mouthwatering finish.

Tricks OF THE TRADE

★ At nighttime, you can afford to go a little over-the-top for fun. Apply a flat, matte shade that's slightly lighter than your skin color under shimmer to make eye shadow last till dawn.

★ **Dark lips won't last long if you apply gloss. If you want a Goth look, wear a dark matte lipstick and skip the gloss.**

★ If you prefer extra-pale lips, apply your concealer over your lips and apply a light colored gloss over the top. The concealer will also help the gloss adhere to your lips.

For a really hot look, choose one feature to *highlight.*

If you want to dazzle with your eyes, go for a smoky eye look. If you choose to make headlines with your pout, reach for a high-impact color like hot pink, red, or gold. Don't let your features compete for attention.

★ If you have the patience and confidence, it can be fun to try new things such as a little glitter on the cheeks, a line of black liquid eyeliner to rim the eyes, or even false eyelashes. It pays to have a practice run before you walk out the door, but once you've test-driven these fun party tricks, you'll be hooked.

THE WAY YOU WEAR

AND APPLY MAKE-UP

WILL NEVER BE

THE SAME AGAIN!

Mood make-up

Mood make-up offers you a revolutionary new way to make up your face and at the same time change your moods and feelings. It's a form of self-healing that's not only fun, it's also a fab way to get in touch with your inner self and unleash the powers of GirlForce.

GO ON, TRY IT!

Ever wonder why blue is your fave color? Or why you hate pink or yellow? In the same way we have preferences for certain foods, we also have instinctive preferences for certain colors. Your Beauty Type not only influences the colors that you'll naturally like and dislike, it also gives you some indication of the colors that will heal and balance your body, mind, and spirit.

According to Ayurveda, everything on the planet can be considered a medicine or a poison depending on your Body Type—foods, sounds, sights, thoughts, ideas, people, plants, places, the list goes on. Air girls, who are sensitive and need pacifying, are healed and balanced with calming, easy-on-the-eye, soft colors like pastel blue and pale lilac. They are disturbed by very bright, violent color such as red and bright purple. Fire chicks, whose natures are passionate and fiery, are soothed and cooled with colors such as aqua or sea green. And Earth babes, who are innately laid-back and low-key, need stimulating colors to give them energy and oomph such as bright orange, cherry red, and gold.

Every time you make up your face, you can balance and heal yourself with color. When you choose your palette of eye shadow, lip color, and blush, be aware that those colors are healing and balancing for your body and soul.

Check out this scenario: You're a Fire girl and you're worried about a big date. You're freaking about what to wear and what style will give you that essential confidence. Then, you put on your cooling pastel make-up—all the while thinking about how the colors are helping you to chill. By the time you have make-up on your face, you're feeling better—less fiery and anxious, more in control and put together like a pro. The right make-up for your Beauty Type not only makes you look like a diva, it helps you feel calm, cool, and collected—just what you want before a big night out!

AIR
COLOR PALETTE

Muted browns are grounding for Air and gold is uplifting.

Try:

- soft, calming pastel pink for lips and cheeks
- pale blue, lilac, and green for eye shadows
- lush pink and orange nail polish

FIRE
COLOR PALETTE

Avoid red, yellow, and brown.

Try:

- cool colors like lime, pale blue, aqua, and white for the eyes
- gorgeous fuchsias and purples for the lips
- dusky pinks and orange for the cheeks
- shimmering pastels for the nails

EARTH
COLOR PALETTE

Avoid wishy-washy pastel shades.

Try:

- warm and stimulating colors such as red, orange, gold, dark brown, and purple
- a slick of berry gloss; your lush mouth will look great

As well as making you look chic and sexy, your make-up colors can change your moods.

Choose a color and alter your feelings

Custom design your own make-up palette, and change your moods too, just by selecting eye shadow, lipstick, nail polish, and blush colors and shades.

WANNA GET CREATIVE AND COOL?

Go for pastel colors: pale pink, pale blue, lilac, soft green, gold, apricot, and glittering shades.

Air colors are uplifting and connect you to your artistic and intuitive powers. When you select an Air color, you'll promote creativity, adventure, a sense of freedom, joy, generosity, intelligence, and psychic awareness.

Go for cool colors: lime, pale blue, aqua, white, cream, dusky pinks, and pale orange.

Fire colors unleash your passionate and courageous side. When you select a Fire color, you'll promote energy, a sense of personal power, confidence, drive, happiness, and enthusiasm.

WANNA GET RELAXED AND ROMANTIC?

Go for warm and stimulating colors: red, orange, gold, dark brown, caramel, olive green, berry, and purple.

Earth colors tap into your romantic and tender essence and help you chill out. When you select an Earth color, you'll promote harmony, balance, patience, fulfillment, sensuality, and a sense of being laid-back and happy to be who you are.

The normal human eye can detect about 150 hues formed by various combinations of the primary colors: red, yellow, and blue.

According to Ayurveda, various colors have the capacity to heal, revitalize, rejuvenate, stimulate, and calm the mind and body.

Red is considered to be a hot, stimulating color, while blue has soothing, calming qualities. Yellow is balancing and harmonizing. Gold is said to bring riches and silver attracts psychic powers and goddess consciousness.

CHAPTER FOUR

A rockin' bod, bring it on!

Head-to-toe pampering and DIY products at your fingertips

Listen up. It's time to shine from the top of your luscious mane to the tips of your polished tootsies. And it doesn't have to take hours or cost you every cent in your piggy bank. These cool recipes and techniques are designed to have you looking your best with minimal fuss. Turn your bathroom into a spa and release the powers of GirlForce.

One of the most indulgent ways to experience GirlForce is to pamper yourself. It's pretty simple, really. When you massage, primp, groom, and take care of yourself, you feel fantastic—and when you feel fantastic, you release GirlForce.

It's not just about having clear skin or lush hair (although we all feel a little better about ourselves when we've got that just-came-out-of-the-salon look); it's also about that inner glow you get when you've put some time and effort into taking care of yourself. It's relaxing and fun to paint your nails, give yourself a facial, or mix up a luxurious beauty treatment. You can also grab a friend and pamper each other.

All the beauty tasks you once thought were a bit mundane and boring, such as washing your hair or wiping off last night's make-up, can be transformed into relaxing and pleasurable GirlForce rituals when you inject awareness into the activity.

So, next time you're shampooing, think about how good it feels to wash the day out of your hair. Notice how much your scalp is enjoying the massage as you work the shampoo into the roots. Then feel the spray of warm water as it cascades over your skin. Suddenly the chore that was washing your hair has been transformed into a nurturing and pampering GirlForce ritual.

It's this awareness that ANYTHING you do in life, from putting on a face mask to strolling on the beach, can become a GirlForce-enhancing activity that's so powerful!

Skin care
from the kitchen

One of the basic principles of Ayurveda is that if you can't eat it, then don't put it on your skin. This may sound a little too green-minded for those of us who love nothing more than slathering on a luxurious cream, but the idea makes sense.

If it's nutritious for my body, it must be good for my skin—

especially for girls with sensitive skin who react to the chemicals in many beauty products. Olive oil, sesame oil, coconut oil, avocado, honey, yogurt, oatmeal, and loads of herbs you find in most kitchens are all considered effective and powerful beauty treatments in Ayurveda.

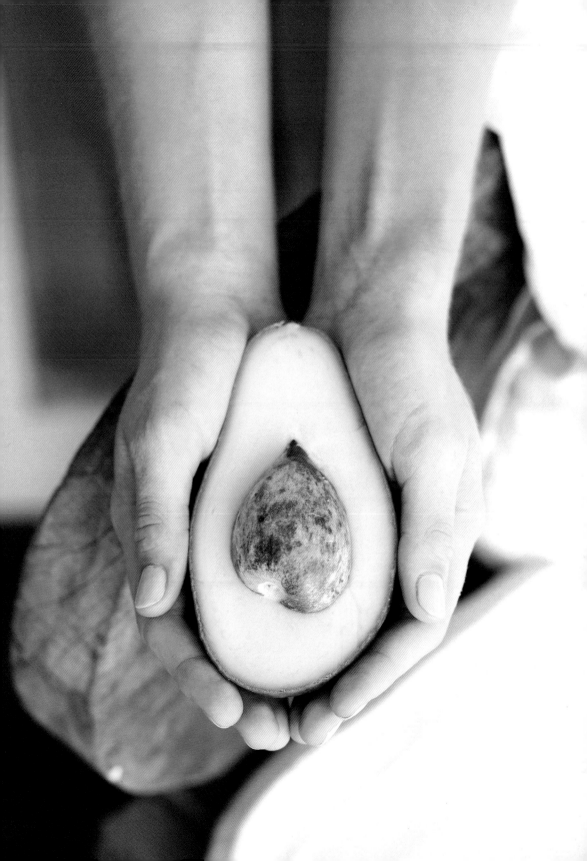

Olive oil is suitable as a face and body moisturizer for all Types and works as an effective conditioner for dry hair.

MIX UP YOUR OWN
yummy skin remedies

- Honey is a soothing all-over moisturizer for the skin and scalp for all Beauty Types. Honey has anti-inflammatory, antibacterial, and anti-infection properties. It can clear rashes, banish zits, smooth away dry skin and dandruff, and leave your skin feeling soft and hydrated. Liquid honey is the easiest to use and it's best applied by using circular movements. If you want to use it as a body moisturizer or scalp treatment, apply it in the shower, leave it on for a few minutes, then rinse well with warm water.

- Pure coconut oil (from health food stores) has natural cleansing properties and works as an effective body moisturizer and hair conditioner. It's cooling and soothing for Fire and nourishing for Air. It's best applied first thing in the morning before showering.

- Apple cider vinegar helps balance the skin and can be used to clean the hair to produce shiny tresses. This is especially beneficial for Air and Earth Beauty Types.

- Rose water is a balancing toner for all Beauty Types, but it's especially good for Earth skins that need toning and tightening.

- Oatmeal makes a great all-over body exfoliation for all Beauty Types; it's fab for dry and sensitive Air skins and leaves a velvety coating on the skin.

- Fresh avocado is a rich and nourishing head-to-toe skin treatment that is especially good for Air and Fire Beauty Types.

- Sesame oil is a warming and nourishing skin and scalp treatment for Air and Earth Types and, as a once-a-week scalp treatment, will help banish dandruff.

- If you can hack it, a teaspoon of freshly squeezed onion juice mixed with half a teaspoon of honey will help get rid of zits anywhere on the body. It's a very traditional Ayurvedic recipe and it works—if your eyes and nose can handle it!

- For bright and radiant skin, mix 2 tablespoons of fenugreek seeds (you can get them from the health food store) and 1 tablespoon of natural yogurt. Soak the seeds in the yogurt for an hour, then blend them into a paste. Gently rub onto the face, neck, back, and chest using circular movements. Leave on the skin for 15 minutes and wash off. Fenugreek is said to be a "miracle spice" that rejuvenates the body and soul.

skin treats

Supernatural face and body cleansers

Draw a bath or turn on the shower and use these delicious skin treats to cleanse your skin. As a once-a-week pampering session, they're a must, but you can also use these recipes to cleanse your skin every day. Become your own beauty therapist!

Air

Mix 3 tablespoons of almond meal with 3 tablespoons of milk and a pinch of sugar. Make a paste in your palm, adding more milk if you want a lighter scrub and more almond meal if you want to get rid of dry, dead cells. Massage gently into the skin and rinse off with warm water.

Fire

Mix 3 tablespoons of almond meal with a teaspoon of grated orange rind and 3 tablespoons of milk. Make a paste in your palm, adding more milk if you want a lighter scrub and more almond meal if you need a deeper clean. Massage gently into the skin and rinse off with cool (not cold) water.

Earth

Mix 3 tablespoons of barley meal with a teaspoon of grated lemon rind and 3 tablespoons of milk. Make a paste in your palm, adding more milk if you want a light scrub and more barley meal if you need a rigorous exfoliation. Massage gently into the skin and rinse off with warm water.

WEEKLY FRUIT-ACID FACE MASK

The naturally occurring acids in fruits and veggies make terrific masks as they deep clean and gently exfoliate the skin.

Mash up the fruit in a bowl, cleanse the skin, and then apply the mask for 10 to 15 minutes. Lie down and relax. Rinse with warm water and apply a moisturizer. The natural acids in the fruit will gently exfoliate your skin so it will feel silky smooth and refreshed.

AIR
- crushed banana or avocado pulp

FIRE
- crushed banana or pineapple pulp

EARTH
- crushed strawberry or papaya pulp

A pampering and relaxing DIY home facial

Give yourself this treatment once a week for radiant skin and a wide, confident smile. Good skin comes from regular pampering and nourishing, and it glows with health when you treat it with the right products and techniques. GirlForce flows when you feel good in your own skin.

Step 1 DEEP CLEAN

After you've covered your bathroom vanity with everything you need for a yummy facial (cleanser, toner, exfoliator, mask, moisturizer, eye cream, lip balm, essential oil, washcloth, eye pads, and towel), cleanse your face as follows.

Fill your sink or a large basin with warm water. Drop in about five drops of a Beauty Type–specific essential oil (see page 57). Soak the washcloth in the warm water and press it all over your skin, deeply inhaling the aroma of the oil. Essential oils have antiseptic properties and will disinfect and cleanse your skin at the same time they relax and calm your emotions.

Then, massage either a foaming cleanser or a creamy cleanser into the skin using small circular motions, and rinse off with the rest of the warm water.

Finally, spritz your skin with an essential oil spray toner (see page 51) or sweep a cotton pad soaked in water over your face and neck.

Step **2**

BUFF
Exfoliating removes the dry, dead surface cells and makes the skin smoother and less prone to dryness and breakouts. A once-a-week buff and polish will keep the skin clean, fresh, and breakout-free.

Step **3**

STEAM

Steaming the skin softens and hydrates it and prepares it for a mask. A few minutes in a warm shower will do the job, but you can also fill a large basin with hot (not boiling) water. Make sure your face is at least eight inches away from the water and place a towel over your head for 5 minutes of steaming. Add a squeeze of fresh lemon juice to refresh the skin and senses. Pat your skin dry.

Step **4**

MASK

This is the part where you get to lie down. Apply a hydrating and soothing mask like a paste of avocado or a slathering of honey and massage it in small circular motions all over your face, neck, and chest. Soak two eye pads in a gentle toner and place them over your eyes.

Or, better still, cut two thin slices of fresh cucumber and place them over each eye. Make sure you lie down for at least 20 minutes to get the full benefits of the time-out. After 20 minutes, rinse your face with cool-to-warm water and pat your face dry with a tissue (it will blot up any excess mask).

Step **5**

MOISTURIZE

Once your face is dry, it's time to nourish your skin with deep, penetrating moisturizers. It's a good idea to use a different product than your normal daily routine to boost the treatment benefits. Don't forget the delicate skin around the eyes, either. (If you can afford a separate eye cream or gel, add it to your treatment routine.) And finally, polish off the treatment by applying a lip balm.

skin types

The texture and condition of your skin will determine the way you adjust your at-home facial. If your skin is dry, oily, or a frustrating combination of both, follow these guidelines to tailor your treatment to your skin's needs.

Dry skin

You may not need to tone your skin if it's super-dry. Avoid alcohol-based toners, which can dry out the skin, and limit your steaming time to just a minute or so.

Acne-prone and oily skin

Exfoliate once a week with a grainy scrub or even every day with a mild exfoliating cleanser. If you have enlarged pores, make sure you cleanse your skin thoroughly and use the lavender compressing technique every day (see page 50).

Combination skin

Figure out where your skin needs moisture (usually the cheeks, forehead, and neck) and where it's oilier (generally the nose, chin, and sometimes the forehead, too) and try using a different mask for the different parts of your face. Go for a clay-based mask for the oily T-zone, as clay absorbs oil and impurities, and opt for a more hydrating mask for the drier parts of your complexion. Be aware that the weather, stress, pollution, and your hormones can change the balance of moisture in your skin.

DOS AND DON'TS

★ Avoid facials if you have a cold sore; it's possible to spread the infection.

★ Always use sunscreen with a high SPF rating if you're using alpha and beta hydroxy acid (AHAs and BHAs) formulas. Products that contain AHAs and BHAs remove the dead cells on the surface of the skin and can make the skin more sun sensitive.

★ Don't over-scrub your skin. Stick to one type of exfoliant, either a chemical peel or a grainy scrub, and do a rigorous treatment only once a week.

★ Don't use scalding-hot water on your skin.

Balance for your hair

You've discovered how to treat your skin. Now it's time to learn how to treat and manage your hair.

Traditionally in India women don't use shampoos or conditioners; they wash their hair with a combination of herbs, oils, fruits, and nuts that naturally purify the scalp and nourish the hair. We won't go that far—it takes a little effort to wash hair this way—but it can be fun (and healthy, too) to treat your hair to some natural hair masks and treatments.

I would encourage you, however, to go for botanically based shampoos and conditioners and avoid products with harsh chemicals such as PEGs (polyethylene glycols, which are often used as lathering agents in shampoos), parabens, and some surfactants such as sodium lauryl sulfate. These chemicals can cause irritations and allergies.

When you wash your hair, treat the experience as an opportunity to pamper yourself. Take in the feel of the water cascading over your hair and scalp and really dive into the enjoyment of taking care of yourself and grooming your luscious locks. This way you get more out of the time spent doing what can be a mundane chore, and you also unleash GirlForce.

Weekly conditioning

HAIR MASK

THE BEST TIME FOR THIS
TREATMENT IS FIRST THING
IN THE MORNING BEFORE
YOUR SHOWER OR LAST
THING AT NIGHT BEFORE
YOU GO TO BED.

Massage your mask into your hair and scalp. The treatment not only helps keep the hair shiny and manageable, it also helps boost the micro-circulation in the scalp and balance oil production. If you want to sleep on it, it's a good idea to protect your sheets with an old towel on your pillow.

Air

Your locks are prone to dryness and can be kinky, unruly, and brittle. Give them a lush, moisturizing treatment with this mask and watch your hair go from dry and dull to shiny and bouncy:

Massage 4 tablespoons of sesame oil into the hair right down to the roots. Wrap your head in a warm towel and leave for 5 to 10 minutes. Wash as normal. Your hair will be luxurious and shiny.

Fire

Your tresses are often thick and shiny with red undertones, and whether they're curly or straight, they're a major part of your look. If your scalp is irritated or your hair is oilier or drier than you'd like it to be, use this nourishing and calming treatment:

Mix 4 tablespoons of avocado oil with five drops of chamomile essential oil and massage into the hair right down to the roots. Wrap your head in a cooled towel (you can put it into the fridge for 10 minutes) and leave for 10 to 15 minutes. Wash as normal with cool water. Your hair will be soft and shiny and your scalp will feel clean and tingly.

Earth

Wavy or straight, your thick crop is a lustrous mass. Sometimes it can get a little greasy, so when it needs a root-to-end cleanse, use this mask:

Combine 4 tablespoons of olive oil, three drops of sage, and three drops of rosemary essential oil and massage into the hair right down to the roots. Wrap your head in a warm towel and leave on for 10 minutes. Wash as normal. The essential oils in this treatment will help balance the sebum in your scalp, which will help control oiliness.

AFTER YOU'VE SHAMPOOED YOUR HAIR, MAKE UP A TEA AND RINSE YOUR HAIR WITH THESE SUBTLE AND NATURAL COLORANTS FROM THE HEALTH FOOD STORE. THEY DON'T CONTAIN ANY HARSH CHEMICALS AND THEY REALLY GIVE YOUR HAIR A GORGEOUS COLOR BOOST!

FOR BLONDE HAIR

Steep half a cup of chamomile flowers in warm water and rinse through the hair.

FOR RED HAIR

Mix a pinch of henna paste with a sprinkling of saffron diluted in warm water and rinse through the hair.

FOR DARK BROWN AND BLACK HAIR

Add a cup of black tea to warm water and rinse through the hair.

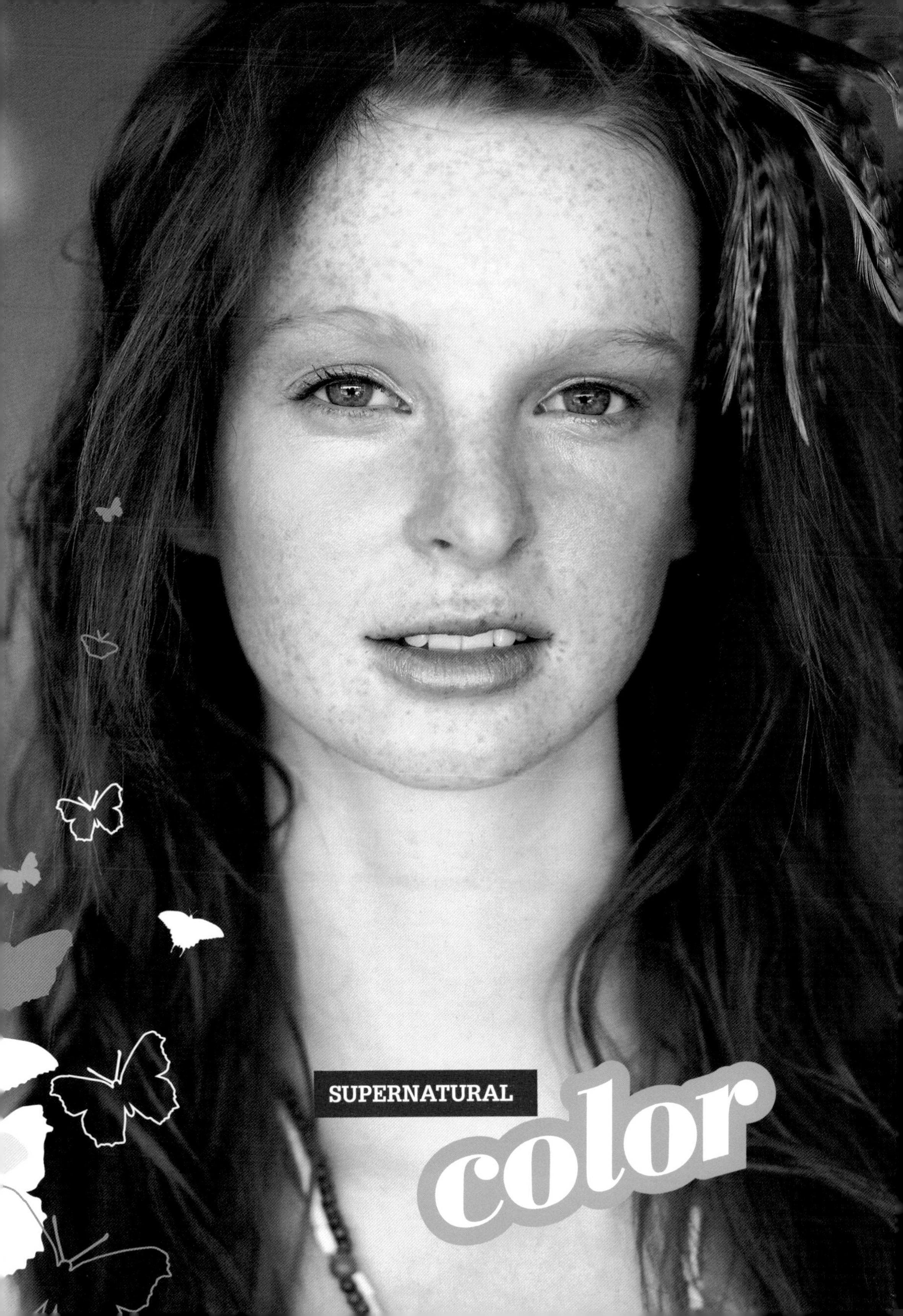
SUPERNATURAL
color

HERE ARE TWO HASSLE-FREE
HAIRSTYLES THAT WILL ADD
SPICE AND GLAMOUR TO BOTH
SHORT AND LONG LOCKS.

The mane event

The formula for great-looking hair is always simple. Get a good cut and use effective products—a moisturizing shampoo and a protective conditioner. Healthy hair looks drop-dead gorgeous whether it's short, long, straight, or curly.

It doesn't matter whether your destination is the mall with your friends or a date with a hottie you've liked forever, you can banish bad hair with a few products, some professional know-how—and a touch of inventiveness.

Don't try too hard to make it perfect.
For a go-anywhere weekend look, simply scrunch some mousse into your hair for volume, add a bobby pin or a headband to give it some oomph, and you're ready to go. For night, weave some braids into your hair and boost it with curls (or go super-straight if you have straight hair). Sparkly barrettes are sassy for night, or go for girlie bows, ribbons, feathers, and jewels for a funky twist.

THE ALICE

Weekend wonderland

If you have long hair, you'll look as pretty as a princess with this style, and if you have short hair you'll look rock-star hot. Rub a quarter-size blob of styling cream onto dry hair, smoothing it from the roots to the ends. Pull your hair back into a messy ponytail and pin it up at the back into a loose bun. Grab three colored ribbons, a strap of leather, or a scarf, and wrap the bands around your head. Secure them at the nape of your neck with some bobby pins. This easy, groovy style gives you instant glamour, even when you're lounging around at home with your pals or off to a low-key BBQ.

Curly girl, night angel.
Wanna look like a disco diva?

Scrunch some mousse or styling cream into dry hair, taking it all the way to the ends. Wrap sections of your hair around a curling iron or rollers.

Once you've done the whole head, leave it for 5 minutes and spray a light mist of a hair spray over the entire head. Take out the rollers (if using). Tip your hair upside down and run your fingers through the curls; this will open them up and make them bouncy.

For a neat twist, part your hair on the side or in the middle and attach a clip or four or five colored bobby pins. Alternatively, you could add braids. Simply section your hair into parts; take a piece at the front, side, or back. Now pull the hair tight and braid it close to the head, weaving in sections from the back to hold it in place. Secure the end with a feather or clip to add color.

This style will make you sizzle.

Styling staples

1. Large Velcro rollers
(to add volume)

2. Small spray bottle
(to spritz the hair with water before adding styling products)

3. Lavender oil
(to clean your hairbrush)

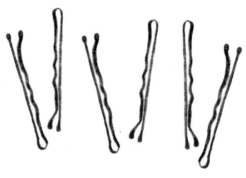

4. Bobby pins
(to secure a twist or add glitz)

5. Bag-size hairbrush
(so you can whip it out when you need it)

6. A stretchy black headband
(when all else fails, push your hair back à la Gwyneth Paltrow)

Dos and Don'ts

- Don't overuse your products; nothing looks worse than stiff, bridesmaid hair.

- Do test; experiment with mousse, gel, cream, wax, pomade, and hair spray and work out which ones give you the most natural hold.

- Don't do mermaid curls; tendrils look oh-so yesterday. Curl your hair in small sections and don't pull the curls down with the curling iron as you release them.

- Don't use alcohol-based hair spray; it dries out the hair.

- Do wash your hair in warm water and do the final rinse with cool water; it will close the hair shaft and make hair look glossy.

FAKE IT

Are you a sun worshipper? Your best bet is to save your skin and grab a tan that comes out of a bottle. Smooth, sun-kissed skin—without streaks or orange stains—is simple when you have the right instructions and tools.

Step **1** **Exfoliate**

In the shower or bath, exfoliate your skin with a loofah or oatmeal scrub. Pay particular attention to the elbows and ankles and make sure you've either shaved or waxed your legs. Towel dry thoroughly and allow the skin to cool down—about 10 minutes. Pull your hair into a ponytail or put it into a shower cap so it won't get in the way. Dab a bit of Vaseline into your belly button to shield it from the tanner.

Step **2** **Apply**

If you've gone for a spray, spritz it onto the skin about six inches away from your bod. If you opted for a cream or gel, squeeze out a handful and in horizontal then vertical strokes, massage it into the skin. Start from your feet and work your way up your body. Make sure you haven't missed any spots, and go lightly over bits that will "grab" the product such as the elbows and knees.

THE ONLY TAN TO GET IS A FAKE TAN

Step 3

Wait and moisturize

Wash your hands with soap as soon as you've finished applying the product. Blot any excess tanner from your knees, ankles, and elbows with a tissue. It's best to let the product soak in for at least an hour, so if you're hanging around the house, sit on an old towel or put on an old pair of sweats and a loose T-shirt. After an hour, apply a moisturizer to "set" the tan. By now you should look sun-kissed and babelicious.

Inside info: self-tanning

☀ Before you choose a self-tanner, test a few brands by making small stripes on your inner arm. Return to the store once the tans have developed. This will help you get the right color for your skin tone.

☀ For a tanned back, grab your best bud and do a duo treatment.

☀ Remove mistakes with soap and water, or, if the tan has developed too far, try a non-acetone nail-polish remover.

☀ To make the tan last, keep moisturizing your body. (As your skin naturally flakes off, you lose the tan.)

☀ Don't forget to wear sunscreen; self-tanner does not protect you from the sun's harmful rays.

Great nails FAST!

STEP-BY-STEP MANICURE

Painting your nails is one fab way to shake up your look. You can go loud with bright colors—and unleash the beauty daredevil within—or you can polish them with pretty pinks and demure pastels and make like a princess. A new look is only a few strokes of color away.

Step 1

SHAPE

If your nails have grown well past your fingertips, they'll need to be clipped before filing—otherwise just file. Clip the tips straight across the tops of your nails so the nails remain square; don't clip the sides. (The strength of the nail comes from the sides, so keeping them square helps stop breakages.)

File off any sharp edges by tilting the emery board under the nail. Stroke in one direction from the sides to the center, not back and forth. Follow by rubbing a buffer over the surface of the nail until it gleams.

SOFTEN

Rub cuticle oil into the cuticles and soak your hands in a bowl of warm water with a splash of olive oil or milk—not soap (it's too drying). After a few minutes, blot your hands dry and gently push back the cuticles using a Q-tip, an orange stick (the wooden stick with a rounded end you see at salons), or a damp towel. Don't cut or trim your cuticles—it can cause infections.

Exfoliate your hands with either a body scrub or some oatmeal in yogurt. Rinse and apply a hand cream.

Step

3

POLISH

Swipe the nails with a non-acetone polish remover. Wipe the polish brush against the edge of the bottle before painting the nails. Brush the color along the center of the nail from base to tip in one even stroke. Repeat on either side of the center stripe. Apply two coats and follow with a layer of quick-drying topcoat. Correct any mistakes with an orange stick or Q-tip dipped in remover.

PEDICURE

Nothing looks better than perfectly polished toenails with strappy sandals or flip-flops. Don't let snaggly toenails get in the way of having sexy show-off feet. This DIY pedi will have your tootsies looking *super-stylish.*

Step 1

PREP
Remove any polish with a non-acetone remover. Clip nails straight across leaving a little bit of nail across the top. Clipping too much from the sides can cause ingrown toenails. File nails into slightly rounded square shapes and dab on an alpha-hydroxy cream or some olive oil.

Step

2

SOFTEN

Rub the soles of your feet with a loofah, foot file, or pumice stone. Soak your feet for 5 minutes in a bowl of warm water and some milk. Gently push back the cuticles with an orange stick, Q-tip, or a damp towel.

Step

3

POLISH

Start by folding a paper towel eight times into a strip and wrapping it around alternate toes to separate them. Paint on the color in three strokes (as with fingernails). Apply two coats and then a quick-drying topcoat. Let them dry for at least an hour.

Inside info: nail know-how

★ Most shades have either a blue or a yellow base. Blue-based shades work best on pale skins while yellow shades tend to suit darker complexions.

★ To choose the right shade for your skin tone, hold the polish bottle next to your inner wrist. You should be able to tell whether the cool bluer tones suit your skin better than the warm yellowish hues or vice versa.

★ If you have a slight chip in your polish, dab remover on your fingertip and rub it over the chip to smooth the edges. Then apply two thin coats of color and a topcoat.

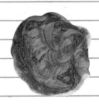

★ A manicure will generally last a week if you're not playing a heavy-duty sport or washing your hands a thousand times a day. A pedicure can last up to three weeks. Applying a topcoat every couple of days will help your mani and pedi last longer.

The nose knows—
The perfect perfume for you

Ever wonder how to pick the right scent for you? With a million scents out there, you are forgiven for being confused. One great way to simplify your choices is to let your Beauty Type be your guide. Smells, like tastes, foods, yoga moves, and even colors, can be either healing or imbalancing for your particular Beauty Type. Check out this list and see which fragrances might suit your tastes.

Air

Unleash your creative and cool side with fresh, citrusy, watery, and green notes that will uplift the senses and set your inventive and artistic side free.

Fire

Unleash your passionate and powerful side with notes such as vanilla, sandalwood, and rich sweet flowers that open up your intense, confident, seductive, and influential traits. They're sassy and go-get-'em.

Earth

Unleash your relaxed and romantic side with woody, earthy scents containing notes such as cedar, oak moss, lavender, and amber. They'll help your laid-back, caring, compassionate, sensuous, and grounded side.

1. Sip a cup of green tea. It's ultra-refreshing and chock-full of skin-caring antioxidants.

2. Give yourself an instant wake-up call with this ancient acupressure technique. With your fingertips, trace the undersides of your collarbone to your sternum. Next, move your fingers about three-quarters of an inch to either side of your chest. Gently massage the two soft spots you feel (known as the K27 acupressure points) to help boost concentration and vitality.

3. Zap a zit by rubbing it with half a clove of fresh garlic. Okay, it's a bit smelly, but the antibacterial agent in garlic helps clear up a pimple.

4. Sleep well and have sweet dreams by spritzing your pillow with lavender essential oil. It calms the nerves and induces peaceful sleep.

5. Have a healthy breakfast and feel revved up for the day. Try oatmeal with yogurt and blueberries—that breakfast combines three super-foods, which help beat a host of imbalances and diseases.

6. Banish puffy eyes. Buy yourself an eye gel and stick it in the fridge.

7. Have a "power shower." Add a few drops of peppermint or sage essential oil to the bottom of the shower and turn on the hot water. The steam will carry the essential oil particles to your nose before you even step in the shower.

8. Give yourself a foot massage and instantly relax. Each morning, apply a soothing foot cream to your feet and rub it in well, concentrating on the arches, the ball of the foot, the toes, and the sides of your feet.

9.   Have a sweet facial. Apply natural organic honey all over your face to smooth away dead skin cells and disinfect any blemishes. Honey has amazing wound-healing properties so it works on an open sore, too.

10.   If you feel a headache coming on, try gathering your hair in bunches, grabbing the roots, and giving three gentle tugs. The action helps relax the muscles that cover the head and scalp, which hold a lot of tension.

11.   Loosen up with a simple stretch. Stand in a doorway and with your palms holding the doorframe, walk through the door, and lean forward. This stretch opens all the chest muscles, stretches the arms and shoulders, and allows you to breathe in deeply.

12.   Boost your energy by squeezing and pulling your ears. Sounds weird, but there are more than 240 acupressure points in your ears and thousands of sensory nerve endings. Squeeze firmly and you'll instantly feel a rush of blood to your ears.

13.   Cleopatra was right: bathing in milk does help your skin feel good. The lactic acid in milk sloughs away dead skin cells and reveals smoother, softer skin.

14.   Don't diet. They don't work, they make you feel depressed, and they can encourage weight gain. If you think you're overweight, talk to your doctor. A professional dietician or nutritionist can help you learn how to eat sensibly. Add in exercise and you'll feel better in next to no time.

15.   Learn to meditate. It's good for your body, mind, and soul—and good for your skin, too. Meditation reduces the amount of the stress hormone cortisol in the blood, which may also help break the acne cycle.

CHAPTER FIVE

Hot looks for everyone

Your Air, Fire, and Earth Beauty Prescription

Okay, so now you have all the tips and techniques at your disposal to positively shine. You've learned how to apply make-up like a pro and fix your hair like a diva. You've also discovered that to glow from the inside out you need to look after yourself, balancing your lifestyle with a little exercise, healthy eating, and plenty of R&R.

Fire

Wanna know how to put it all together? Here's how. Follow these simple guidelines for balancing Air, Fire, and Earth and you'll not only unleash the full-tilt powers of GirlForce, you'll also look and feel fab.

Ready to launch into your new regimes of pampering and beautifying? Cool. Before you start, there's something I really want you to understand: celebrating yourself just the way you are means being unconditionally loving and compassionate with yourself—but it also means making time to take care of yourself.

Accepting yourself is a holistic process. It's about embracing your whole self—your body, mind, and spirit inside and out. When you accept yourself, and stop any negative self-talk, you can grow and evolve as a person. Self-acceptance should not be confused with self-neglect.

We all have days when we just want to hang around in our sweats and let our grooming slip. That's fine, in fact it's more than fine; it's essential to let yourself off the hook sometimes. However, it's not okay to eat junk food constantly, sit like a blob on the couch watching TV, and let your hair go greasy and your nails go ragged. That's self-neglect and it's a sign that you DON'T love and accept yourself.

The reason it's vital to pamper and groom yourself is that it makes you feel good and it makes the world regard you in a respectful way. If you have self-respect, you'll attract respect from the people around you.

GirlForce is about lifting your game. It's about making the most of what you've got. It's about injecting love and passion into every aspect of your life, including your schoolwork, your grooming, your exercise, your relationships, and your body, mind, and spirit. GirlForce is not about living in a halfhearted way; it's about taking on life with energy, power, and confidence.

When you take care of yourself, you increase your confidence levels.

Who doesn't need more confidence? The answer? Nobody. It takes a little effort to groom and pamper ourselves, but when we do we not only look great but we tap into the mega-confidence-boosting powers of GirlForce.

Go on girl,

get out there and shine

I wrote this book (and the first GirlForce
book) as a way to spread good karma.
As someone who has spent more than a
decade being a beauty editor, this book
is probably closest to my heart. I know
from experience that when you put
energy and love into looking good, it sets
in motion the magical universal principle
of "like increases like"—it means that
when you feel your best, better things
come to you. Believe in this magic and
anything is possible.

Guidelines for *balancing air*

As an Air Beauty Type you are one clever chick. Blessed with a quick mind and an incredible capacity for joy and generosity, you're an inspiration. Air girls have a powerful imagination and they're generally the most artistic of all three types. They're revolutionaries who need to run their own race—natural rebels who dislike overbearing authority figures and too much routine.

Air babes are sensitive and can be vulnerable. You may fantasize a lot, and your daydreams can be a great escape. You're as likely to become a pop idol and invent a new craze as you are to become a spiritual seeker sitting on a mountain contemplating your navel. You're the girl who doesn't like rules and wants to invent her own way to be.

Air

Earth

Fire

When it comes to your beauty concerns, it's fair to say that you're not too good at sticking to routines.

Good advice for Air girls is to keep it simple. Maintain a basic skin, hair, and nail routine and keep everything as neat and tidy as possible (you're not the girl with neat hair, so it will take a little effort to tame your tresses). Use healing, grounding, and soothing essential oil–based skin and hair care and get plenty of rest and sleep—it's easy for you to deplete your energy and you can end up feeling anxious and exhausted.

Beauty Type beautiful

- Air has cold, dry qualities so warm, moist, nourishing foods such as stews, creamy curries, and oatmeal have a beneficial effect on your bod.

- Sweet, soothing foods such as pudding, soups, hot cereals, hot chocolate, and freshly baked breads are good for calming the sometimes anxious Air Type.

- Air girls are easily disturbed and have a sensitive demeanor. It's important for Air girls to create a calm, quiet atmosphere as often as possible.

- Do a little yoga, Tai Chi, or gentle exercise such as walking every day.

- Listen to soothing and calming music (heavy metal disturbs you).

- Use heavier creams and oils to treat your skin, which can be a little on the dry side.

- Nourish your nails (which can be brittle) by bathing them in a bowl of olive oil.

- Don't over-wash your hair—it tends to be dry, so use a rich conditioner and wash only when it's dirty. Style with non-drying creams and pomades and avoid alcohol-based gels.

- Wear soft pastel make-up shades and stick to lighter colors for your wardrobe (black can make Air girls dark and depressed).

- Learn to meditate to calm your body, mind, and spirit.

- Practice daily confidence-boosting affirmations.

Guidelines for *balancing fire*

One of the first things anyone will notice about a Fire babe is her personal power and charisma. You have the ability to win friends and influence people. Fire girls are courageous, ambitious, and motivated. You can change the world if you want to. You like to be the center of attention but you don't need to try too hard to have a circle of admirers around you—your natural powers of attraction do that for you.

Sometimes you can be a little too focused and you may be accused of being arrogant. It's cool to be confident, but sometimes it's also good to be compassionate about people who are not as fortunate as you. You may not think you're as drop-dead gorgeous as some girls, but you have an energy and enthusiasm for life that makes you magnetic.

YOUR MOTTO

I'm feisty and fiery, I'm passionate and driven— accept me as I am. I'm a girl on the move and I'm going places.

When it comes to your beauty concerns, you are probably going to say that zits, redness, and irritations are high on your list. Fire girls often get red, irritated zits and find they get very flushed, especially in summer. You're good at sticking to routines (even though patience is not your strong suit), so check out how to balance Fire with the right foods, exercise, mind powers, and skin regimes and you'll get great results in next to no time.

TO STAY
Beauty Type beautiful

🍀 The most important principle for the Fire vixen is to keep cool, particularly in summer.

🍀 Fire girls generally have naturally strong digestive systems. As a result, Fire girls can take their bodies for granted and eat more than they should. It's important for Fire girls not to eat too much too quickly, or to go overboard with sodium, caffeine, or fried foods.

🍀 Excessive Fire tends to make the body sour (think smelly breath and perspiration). To prevent this, Fire gals should take extra care with hygiene and teeth cleanings.

🍀 Do a little cooling and calming exercise daily such as swimming, yoga, Pilates, or walking.

🍀 Learn to meditate.

🍀 Do something kind for someone every day— it teaches compassion.

🍀 Listen to romantic music to keep your moods sweet and happy.

🍀 Wear pretty pinks, bright white, and feminine make-up colors and ensure your clothes are also bright, pretty colors—it will keep you feeling empowered and radiant.

🍀 Wear sunscreen daily.

🍀 Stick to a routine of pure botanical skin care and cleanse, tone, and moisturize regularly.

🍀 Take care of your hair with effective products that promote shine and vibrant color. If you have red or blonde hair, opt for products that bring out your natural highlights.

Guidelines for *balancing earth*

You are the faithful friend, devoted girlfriend, loving daughter and sister. You have a natural ability to love and show compassion to everyone. Your friends lean on you and you get compliments about your easy-going nature. You are generally lush—you have abundant hair, large soulful eyes, and a voluptuous bod. You're all girl, baby!

Femininity is a true Earth trait and your curves are a testament to your gender.

You are a lover of beauty and you like harmony in your environment and in your internal world. You are romantic and may sometimes be accused of being a dreamer. You're not fast to act; in fact, you're deliberate and can be slow to make up your mind. However, once you've committed to something, you have real endurance and staying power. You are a dreamy girl who will spread good vibes with your tenderness and kindness.

Laid-back and lush, I'm a dreamy girl with a tender, loving heart.

When it comes to your beauty concerns, you feel like you've got a list as long as your arm— you're curvier than most, sometimes taller than the average, and can get greasy skin and hair and the odd nasty zit. Confidence is not always your best friend. But hold on, girl, what you do have is fabulous— healthy skin, gorgeous hair, strong teeth and nails, and a robust sense of self. Stimulate your bod and mind with a regular healing dose of get-off- your-butt exercise and you'll feel powerful and in control in an instant.

Beauty Type beautiful

★ **Overeating is the Achilles' heel of the Earth girl. The best Earth-balancing foods are light, dry, and warm and have mostly spicy, bitter, and astringent tastes (like tea and asparagus). In fact, bitter and astringent tastes help curb your appetite.**

★ Eat meals made up of low-fat foods, lightly cooked vegetables, and sour fruits.

★ Spices such as ginger, turmeric, pepper, garlic, cinnamon, and paprika help stimulate your slow digestive system.

★ Eat fewer cold, sweet, and heavy tastes and textures. For example, ice cream is not a balancing food for Earth.

★ Do regular, stimulating exercise such as tennis, jogging, aerobics, or some form of power yoga.

★ Keep your skin in great condition by doing regular home facials.

★ Use stimulating essential oils in your skin care to banish zits and uplift your moods and emotions.

★ Occasionally change your beauty routine and add in something exciting and new like a trip to the beauty salon. Earth girls need to shake things up a bit to keep life interesting.

★ Wear sunscreen.

★ Give yourself regular self-massages with a loofah or dry brush.

★ Don't get too cold. It makes Earth girls feel withdrawn and miserable.

★ Get loads of fresh air and spend time in nature. This will help stimulate your mind and uplift your spirits.

★ Treat your hair to a good conditioner—one that's not too heavy—and don't over-wash your hair; it can produce more oil.

★ Learn to meditate and do regular confidence-boosting affirmations.

Connect to the Power!

It doesn't matter if you're not drop-dead gorgeous or the most popular girl in your class. You can feel bulletproof every day by simply connecting to your own internal power source—your GirlForce.

GirlForce is many things—power, confidence, compassion, growth, stamina, vitality, joy, and bliss—but mostly it manifests in our hearts and souls as our human ability to love.

Taking care of yourself is a way to express self-love. It's an exercise in confidence and self-respect. By pampering and primping every day, you make your grooming rituals into a meditation on GirlForce.

Look into the mirror, smile, and allow yourself to adore the person looking back at you. I promise, she's the most beautiful girl in the world—she's unique, lovable, and special.

She's you

CREDITS

This book is dedicated to all the girls who have loved and supported GirlForce—you SHINE!

This book could not have come together without the incredible work of an amazing team of creative and talented people:

My deepest thanks go to Steven Chee, a supremely sensitive and inspired photographer with a heart of gold. Also thanks to Katie Nolan and Dan Nadel: you guys rock. Nadene Duncan did the brilliant styling for the book—honey, you're an angel, love your work. From the bottom of my heart, I thank Kimberley Forbes, who did the most beautiful make-up I've ever seen with such grace and style. Also thanks to hair maverick Hanna Lynch.

A massive thank you to the models for this book—the beautiful SHINE competition winners! The sweet Air girls, Yasmin Suteja and Beata Khaidurova; the feisty Fire girls, Alia Pretzil and Lauren Sedger; and the lush Earth girls, Martina Pasqualino and Kat Bradley. Thank you to the SHINE girls' parents, who accompanied them on the shoot and gave their support so generously to me and the project. Also thanks to the professional models, Natalie Jayne Rosser from Chic; Jessica McColl, Katie Dunkley, and Charlotte Barge from Work; Autumn Armstrong and Mikki Tracton from Vivien's Model Management; and Ortenzia Borreggine from Platform Models—you girls were a dream to work with.

Words can't express my thanks to Lucy Isherwood and Nerida Orsatti, the awesome designers of this book. Your professionalism and extraordinary talent deserve the highest praise.

Finally, my love and thanks go to Rowan Jacob, my partner in GirlForce and life—you and Liberty are my world.

I must also give a big cheer to the ABC for having the trust and faith in me to bring this amazing project together. Thanks to my lovely, patient, and compassionate publishers, Belinda Bolliger and Stuart Neal. Also thanks to Megan Drinan for your gentle editing.